LEGAL ISSUES JOURNAL

Volume 5, Issue 1
January 2017

LEGAL ISSUES JOURNAL

Volume 5, Issue 1
January 2017

Legal Issues is an international journal managed and published by the UK Law and Society Association (UKLSA). The Journal publishes fine research in all fields of law on the basis of its contribution to the society, originality, interdisciplinary interest, and quality. Every effort has been made to ensure accuracy of the submissions. However, the UKLSA is not responsible for any errors. The views expressed in this journal are those of the authors and do not necessarily reflect those of the Editorial Board or of the UKLSA. We are therefore unable to accept responsibility for the content of the submissions.

To advertise with Legal Issues Journal, email the Editor-In-Chief (editor@uklsa.co.uk) or visit www.legalissuesjournal.com.

The United Kingdom Law and Society Association

www.uklsa.co.uk

Table of Contents

Copyright Protection of Fictional Characters in Films: U.K. and U.S. Perspectives

Bashayer Al-Mukhaizeem[1]

Copyright law grants a commercial monopoly over original expression embodied in fictional characters for a specific time. Thus, the copyrightability of created characters depends on their originality. However, free speech, fair use, and the public domain should not be affected by copyright protection. Conversely, the ideas which the characters are based on are outside the sphere of copyright protection. Problematically, it is not always easy to draw a clear, consistent line distinguishing between the elements of fictional characters which are protected, and those which are not. This paper scrutinises the U.K. and the U.S. Jurisprudence in order to clarify their perspectives on this matter.

Key words: Copyright protection - fictional characters - films - idea/expression dichotomy.

---

[1]LLM in Information Technology and Intellectual Property Rights, University of Sussex; LLM in International Commercial Law, University of Sussex; LLM in Private Law, University of Kuwait; Senior Legal Researcher in Civil Service Commission of Kuwait.

1. Introduction

Fictional characters are regarded as valuable commodities. Copyright protection provides the creators of fictional characters with a legal tool to exclude others from using, exploiting, abusing and reaping financial benefits from their fictional characters for a limited duration of time.[2] Copyright only protects the physical elements of the work, such as creative expressive characters, whereas invisible intellectual inspiration is unprotected. This is known as the idea/expression dichotomy,[3] which is applied to determine which aspects of a character are subject to copyright protection. Consider, for example, a film that depicts a celebration of a marriage between a rabbit and a giraffe. The writer intended to refute racism through the portrayal of the marriage between the 'long' giraffe and the 'short' bunny. In this case, using similar appearance with the writer's unique shape of characters, i.e. bunny and giraffe, will probably constitute copyright infringement. This is the case even if the infringing medium is different, such as writing a play with the same characters, and even if the story is based on a totally different subject matter. However, using characters with identical general attributes and the idea of combating racism in another film with real characters as an illustration may not infringe copyright law.

Authors use their imagination to cover an idea with an expressive character with distinct attributes.[4] The author uses his thoughts to characterise specific characters and hence, he is the one who exploits the economic benefit of such characters.[5] This is guaranteed through copyright protection, which prevents third parties from misappropriating the characters.[6] If you are of the

[2]Feldman, 'Finding a Home for Fictional Characters: A Proposal for Change in Copyright Protection' (1990) 78 California Law Review, 689.

[3]Smith, 'The Limits of Copyright: Property, Parody and the Public Domain' (1993) 42(6) Duke Law Journal, 1243.

[4]Biswas, 'Copyrightability of Characters' (2004) 9Journal of Intellectual Property Rights, 148.

[5]Ibid, 148.

[6]Ibid.

1970s or '80s generation, you will probably remember *The White Lion*, a Japanese animated series which proximally resembles *The Lion King*. This resemblance is unlikely to be a coincidence.[7] It is true that the story is different, but the characters are distinctly similar. For example, *Scar* in *The Lion King* and *Bubu* in *The White Lion* are both dark and have a peculiar left eye.[8] The characters' names are similar too: for instance, *Simba* and *Kimba*.[9] A letter supplemented with a petition signed by many Japanese artists was sent to *Disney*. The creators of *The Lion King* claimed that they knew nothing about the existence of *The White Lion*. The producers of *The White Lion* did not pursue legal action against *Disney*.[10] If they did so, it is highly likely that the Japanese producers would win the lawsuit.

Despite the aforementioned points, the law in the area of fictional characters is, to a large extent, uncertain and confusing because the courts' decisions are neither predictable nor consistent[11] in both the U.K. and the U.S. jurisdictions. Neither the U.S. Copyright Act nor U.K. laws provide an explicit protection for fictional characters. There are different opinions about which category of copyright fictional characters can be classified in. These suggestions are explained in the next section.

2. Fictional Characters versus Artistic Works

The U.S. Copyright Act provides protection to, among others, pictorial and graphic works, motion pictures and other audio visual works.[12] In order to protect film characters from imitation and ex-

---

[7]The Japanese version was called 'The Jungle Emperor'.

[8]Kuwahara, 'Japanese Culture and Popular Consciousness: Disney's The Lion King vs. Tezuka's Jungle Emperor' (1997) 31(1) The Journal of Popular Culture, 38-39.

[9]Ibid, 38-39.

[10]Ibid, 40.

[11]Said, 'Fixing Copyright in Characters: Literary Perspectives on a Legal Problem' (2014) 35 Cardozo Law Review, 772.

[12]U.S. Copyright Act 1976 s 102(a)(5)(6).

ploitation, they are likely required to be original.[13] U.S. Copyright Act defines audio visual works as a:

> ...series of related images which are intrinsically intended to be shown by the use of machines, or devices such as projectors, viewers, or electronic equipment...regardless of the nature of the material objects, such as films or tapes, in which the works are embodied.[14]

There are three requirements in order to protect fictional character in the U.S., namely: 1) the character should be original; 2) the character should be regarded as an expressive work, and; 3) the work should be embodied in a tangible medium, which, in our case, is a film.[15] Originality means not only independent work which is not copied from others, but also work that should be, to some extent, unique and unfamiliar.[16] Thus, in the U.S., films are regarded as audio visual works and could be categorised as works of art.

Some commentators argue that fictional characters cannot be considered as artistic works on the basis that the characters' traits are not only depicted by drawings, but also from their behaviour and conduct throughout the film.[17] For example, *Cinderella*'s personality is peaceful and kind, and cannot be perceived in someone's mind unless watching the film. In *United Artists v. Ford Motor,* the plaintiff claimed that *Ford* used the plaintiff's character, the *Pink Panther,* in its car commercials.[18] The court ruled that the animated cat featured in *Ford* advertisements was not qualitatively and substantially similar to the *Pink Panther*, thus, *Ford* was not an infringer. The courts refused to resort merely to the similarity in

---

[13]Ibid.

[14]U.S. Copyright Law and Related 1976 Title 17(101).

[15]Petridis, 'Comparative Issues on Copyright Protection for Films in the U.S. and Greece' (2014) 19*Journal of Intellectual Property Rights*,283.

[16]Ibid, 283.

[17]Biswas, *op. cit.,* 149.

[18]*United Artists Corp. v. Ford Motor Co.,* 483 F. Supp. 89 [1980].

the physical appearance of the two characters. Instead, the court decided the case according to the characters' personalities, movement, colours and the music they were accompanied by.

Some commentators argue that the court should resort to the misappropriation of using a character similar to the *Pink Panther* rather than the detailed features of both characters.[19] In *Warner Bros. v. American Broadcasting,* the court found that *Ralph Hinkely* was not infringing on the basis that there was no substantial similarity to *Superman.*[20] The court resorted to 'the total perception' test, which depends not only on the physical resemblance between the two characters, but also on the characters' attributes in the film. The approach of the court was plot-directed, thus the fictional characters in some cases cannot have an independent character as such apart from the storyline of the film. Thus, it cannot be regarded as an artistic work. However, when the first version of *Mickey Mouse* was created, the character was roguish, drinking beer and smoking. Thereafter, he was illustrated as a boyish and meek personality imparted with a sense of adventure.[21] Thus, the character acquired new characterisation over the years. This indicates that a character can exist independently from a film, and then could constitute an artistic work. In *Walt Disney v. Air Pirates*, the court held that copying only the appearance of *Disney* characters outside the scope of their plot in film, i.e. without copying their characterisation in the storyline of a film, could constitute copyright infringement.[22]

The prerequisite of originality is probably not a requirement under U.K. jurisprudence. Fictional characters could be considered, according to the Copyright, Designs and Patents Act 1988, which was extracted from British copyright law,[23] either as: 1) a drawing

---

[19]Feldman, *op. cit.,* 697.

[20]720 F.2d 231 [1983].

[21]'Western Animation / Mickey Mouse'. <http://tvtropes.org/pmwiki/pmwiki.php/WesternAnimation/MickeyMouse?from=Main.MickeyMouse> accessed 9 April 2016.

[22]*Walt Disney Productions v. Air Pirates* 581 F.2d 751 C. A. Cal. [1978].

[23]Bently, and Sherman, *Intellectual Property Law* (Oxford, OUP 2014), 31.

or painting, where originality is a requirement; or 2) a part of a film, where originality is not a requirement. However, the characters in a film script, which is regarded as a literary work, should be original.

3. Originality and Fictional Characters

In the U.K.[24] and the U.S. alike, there is a requirement of originality in order to protect expressive works in general.[25] Copyright law only protects original expressions which are not copied by others.[26] In a U.S. case, *Feist*,[27] it was held that copyrightability depends on originality. It was stated that the threshold of creativity is very low. Thus, novel aspects of characters are not pursued: if copyrighted fictional characters possess a 'minimal degree of creativity' or 'some creative spark', then that would be sufficient.[28]

A fictional character could either be an idea, which reflects a general concept, or an expression, which embodies a detailed development of an idea.[29] Copyright does not protect basic facts,[30] on the grounds that there is no expression in facts, which are considered synonymous with ideas. If a fictional character's catchphrase is 'life is short, do whatever you like', such a simple factual phrase could become a part of a character, but it is unlikely that it could be protected. However, a character's more distinc-

---

[24] *University of London Press Ltd v. University Tutorial Press Ltd.* 2 Ch 601 [1916].

[25] Ang, 'The Idea-Expression Dichotomy and Merger Doctrine in Copyright Laws of the U.S. and the U.K.' (1994) 2(2) International Journal Law Information Technology, 126.

[26] Bently & Sherman, *op. cit.,* 94.

[27] *Feist Publications, Inc., v. Rural Telephone Service Co.* 499 U.S. 340 [1991].

[28] Kellogg, 'The Problem of Fictional Facts: Idea, Expression and Copyright's Balance between Author Incentive and Public Interest' (2011) 58 Journal of the Copyright Society of the U.S.A., 561.

[29] Helfand, cited Leon Kellman, *op. cit.,* 624.

[30] Bently & Sherman, *op. cit.,* 95.

tive motto, such as 'life is but a story and you are the author', might be copyrighted as an idiosyncratic part of a character.

Each fictional character possesses two different components, namely the developed creative aspect of a copyrighted character, and the character's abstract outline, which is unprotected.[31] In *Detective comics v. Bruns*, the court held that *Superman's* qualities, such as being a hero archetype, wearing a cloak and being benevolent, should be considered as ideas, and ideas are outside of the scope of copyright.[32] Moreover, the court considered that neither choosing the word 'man' in the defendant's character, *Wonderman*, nor developing the powers of *Superman*, is infringing, because they reflected the meaning of an idea. Thus, these characteristics are not protected against copying. However, specific details of the strips are regarded as particular expression, which does enjoy legal protection.[33] Developed portrayals and detailed descriptions of *Superman* do not merely constitute a delineation of a philanthropic hero, but embody original expressions, which are subjected to copyright protection. The plaintiff is not entitled to monopolise normal features of *Superman* such as beneficence to humankind or feats of strength. Thus, the court concluded that *Wonderman* infringed the copyright of *Superman* as a result of copying more than the general features of *Superman*.[34]The idea of a character will not be transformed into an expression unless the character is sufficiently described to reflect the meaning of uniqueness, distinctiveness and individuality of such a character. Only then will the character be an original expression and not merely an idea, and will therefore be protected.[35]

Based on the above, before applying the protection, the issue of whether or not the character is original, expressive and well delineated enough to be protected by copyright should be scrutinised, in addition to whether or not the imitated character is sub-

---

[31]Petridis, *op. cit.*, 286.

[32]*Detective Comics, Inc. v. Bruns Publications, Inc.*, 111 F.2d 432 2d Cir. [1940].

[33]Ibid.

[34]Ibid.

[35]Biswas, *op. cit.*, 150-151.

stantially similar to the authentic one. If yes, the subsequent character infringes copyright of the pre-existing character.[36] In *Mattel v. MCA*, *Mattel* brought an action against *MCA Records*' song, *Barbie Girl*.[37] *Barbie* is a character used in many series and films. However, it might be difficult to rely on copyright to protect *Barbie's* character, her boyfriend and her car, on the basis that they might not be creative enough to be protected. They merely represent normal character shapes of daily life. 'No one may claim originality as to facts'[38] on the grounds that the origin of facts does not stem from authorship.[39] In U.K. jurisprudence, the unauthorised reproduction of the *Barbie* character in a video clip by a third party may not infringe copyright, as several U.K. cases did not rely on the substantial similarities between the characters, which merely reflect normal features of facts.[40] However, according to U.K. jurisprudence, the author should exercise intellectual qualities in order to reach the originality threshold, namely labour, skill or judgment. If *Barbie* required a substantial amount of labour, the work may be considered as an original protected work. Notwithstanding, some scholars assert that copying or merely depicting a normal idea in a character may not constitute an original work, even if it required technical drawing of such a character,[41] because such labour is irrelevant. Others state that the important thing is labour exercised regardless of the creativity or ingenuity aspect,[42] as the aim is to not permit others 'to reap where they have not sown'[43]

Nevertheless, a reproduction of *Barbie* merely relying on *Barbie* as inspiration and copying the subject matter of *Barbie's* character, is unlikely to be protected, irrespective of the use of the word

---

[36]Feldman, *op. cit.,* 691.

[37]*In Mattel, Inc. v. MCA Records, Inc.*, 296 F.3d 894 9th Cir. [2002].

[38]*Feist, op. cit.*

[39]Kellogg, *op. cit.,* 561.

[40]Bently & Sherman, *op. cit.,* 97-98.

[41]Ibid.

[42]Rahmatian, 'Originality in U.K. Copyright Law: The Old "Skill and Labour" Doctrine under Pressure' (2013) 44(1) International Review of Intellectual Property and Competition Law, 12.

[43]Ibid, 12.

Barbie as a trademark. This conclusion is derived from a U.K. case, *Bauman v. Fussell.*[44] However, in another U.K. case, *Ladbroke,* it was noted that individual parts may not be original and, therefore, not protected by copyright, but the compilation of the parts as a whole may be considered as an original work. [45] Thus, although *Barbie* may reflect the ordinary character of a blond girl, her style of clothing, eye colour, makeup, smile and body measurements could constitute an original character. At the same time, according to U.S. law, it is unlikely that a fictional character that reflects the normal features of facts will be protected. The purpose of the originality prerequisite is to prove that the work reflects the authors' personality, excluding objective elements of the work, such as functions, facts and ideas.[46]

In a U.S. case, *DC Comics v. Mark Towle*, the court decided that the plaintiff had copyright exclusivity over the *Batmobile*, and the sale of replicas of it by the defendant constituted copyright infringement.[47] The *Batmobile* is recognisable and has physical and conceptual distinctiveness, such as high-tech features, weaponry, and *Batman* details. Thus, it is not merely a stock character. The *Batmobile* possesses consistent fundamental features whenever it appears, despite the changes in its look over the years, which incorporate up-to-date weaponry and technology elements.[48] The author has the exclusive right to authorise a third party to create a derivative work based on the copyrighted character.[49] It could be argued, as was concluded in *Bezpečnostní*, that the originality of the expressive *Batmobile* could not be achieved as long as it was dictated by the technical functions of the film.[50] In other words, the plot of the *Batman* movie required a fast car equipped with weapons to confront enemies, and thus,

---

[44]*Bauman v. Fussell* 1953 CA [1978].

[45]*Ladbroke Ltd v. William Hill* 1 WLR 273 [1964].

[46]Bently & Sherman, *op. cit.,* 95.

[47]*DC Comics v. Mark Towle*, 802 F.3d 1012 9th Cir. [2015].

[48]Ibid.

[49]Makulilo, 'Holy Copyright Law, Batman! The Batmobile is a copyright Character' (2016) 11(1) Journal of Intellectual Property Law & Practice, 13-14.

[50]*Bezpečnostní Softwaro v. á Asociace* C-393/09 [2010].

there is no room for the author to freely express his creativity in depicting the car. Therefore, this car may not reflect the author's thoughts, but instead was amenable according to the scenario of the film. Hence, the *Batmobile* could be protected as a part of the copyrighted film but not as an independent entity.

This conclusion is drawn by analogy to the *Football Association Premier League* case. In that case, the court refused to regard a football match as an intellectual creation on the basis that matches are subject to the game rules and there is no room for freedom to demonstrate creativity or an author's personality.[51] But *Batmobile* did not merely follow the plot of the film. The details used in the car dramatically reflected the notion of uniqueness and how the creator employed *Batman's* distinctive characteristics in a car. Thus, *Batmobile* does not merely represent the functional elements required to fulfill the scenario, it also transcends them. Nevertheless, it is unlikely to be regarded as a copyrighted sculpture as the underlying purpose of the three-dimensional *Batmobile* is not merely to possess a visual appeal, but to be driven as a part of a film to distinguish *Batman*. Thus, the function is utilitarian rather than purely aesthetic.[52] This conclusion is reached by analogy with a U.K. case, *Lucasfilm v. Ainsworth*. In that case, the court held that a helmet, which was used in a film, was not considered to be a sculpture.[53] The *Batmobile* and other fictional characters are readily available to be used by the public when such characters enter the public domain, as the next section will show.

4. Fictional Characters and Public Domain

The public domain embraces materials that are unprotected by copyright law, either because they fall out of the sphere of copyright protection, such as characters that merely reflect normal

---

[51] *Football Association Premier League & Others v. QC Leisure & Others* C-403/08 [2011].

[52] Bently & Sherman, cited Mann *op. cit.*, 76-77.

[53] *Lucasfilm Ltd v Ainsworth* EWCA Civ 1328 [2009].

ideas without any distinctive impression, or because the protected duration of legislative monopoly of the distinctive characters has expired. For example, fiction featuring the famous detective *Sherlock Holmes* was first published before 1923 and is, therefore, in the public domain. Thus, other authors are free to write their own *Sherlock Holmes* series.[54]Copyrighted characters can become free to the public 70 years after the author's death.[55] Hence, copyright underpins the public domain through the limited monopoly of unique characters and excludes indistinctive characters. This support of the public domain by copyright law has the impact of promoting creativity by presenting raw material that can be used to create imaginative characters.[56] The owner of an unexpired character has exclusivity on reproducing,[57] distributing the character to the public,[58] showing a performance of the character,[59] adapting the shape of the character[60] and authorising others to perform any of the aforementioned restricted acts.[61] The exclusive rights of the author give the public the opportunity to see high-quality reproductions of fictional characters, as poor reproductions provide an unappealing image of the original work.[62] Notably, even during the monopolised period for exploiting creative characters, the audience is permitted to use such characters without the owner's consent.[63] This can be done under the doc-

---

[54]Liu, 'The New Public Domain' (2013) 4 University of Illinois Law Review, 1445.

[55]Copyright, Designs and Patents Act 1988 (CDPA) s 12(2). Helfand, *op. cit.,* 629.

[56]Kuhne, 'The Steadily Shrinking Public Domain: Inefficiencies of Existing Copyright Law in the Modern Technology Age' (2004) 50 Loyola Law Review, 555.

[57]CDPA s 17.

[58]Ibid*,* s 18 & Council Directive 93/83/EEC of 1993 Ch II, art 2.

[59]Ibid*,* s 19.

[60]Ibid*,* s 21.

[61]Ibid*,* s 16(2).

[62]Allan, 'After Bridgeman: Copyright, Museums and Public Domain Works of Art' (2007) 155(4) University of Pennsylvania Law Review, 982.

[63]Smith, *op. cit.,* 1245-1247.

trine of fair dealing, such as for the purpose of performing research, private study, reporting current events, criticism and review, or for non-profit cultural or religious purposes.[64] In the U.K. and the U.S., a defendant can refute the violation of a copyrighted character by resorting to the defence of fair use. It considers the purpose of the use of characters, in particular, whether the characters were used for non-profit or commercial purpose. The court also considers the substantiality of the copyrighted part used in relation to the character, and the effect of the use on the value of the character.[65] If a character lacks an influential element on the film, it may not be protected and, thus, it will remain in the public domain for others' exploitation. This will be elaborated in the following section.

5. Fundamentality of Fictional Characters

Copyrighted characters can be used freely without reimbursing the author[66] when the character does not have an impact on the work as a whole.[67] Consequently, characters in 'character-driven works', such as *Friends*, are more likely to be protected than those in 'plot-driven works', such as *E.R.*[68] This is because characters in *Friends* represent the story and without such characters the story cannot be told. In contrast, in *E.R.*, where the characters are only elements of the narrative and, thus, the story can be told

[64]Madi, 'Mash-Up Songs: Are There Any Exceptions to the Exclusive Rights in the Light of the Jordanian Copyright Protection and Related Rights Law?' (2015) 18(3) The Journal of World Intellectual Property, 91-92.

[65]Chatelain, 'Harry Potter and the Prisoner of Copyright Law: Fan Fiction, Derivative Works, and the Fair Use Doctrine' (2012) 15 Tulane Journal of Technology and Intellectual Property, 206.

[66]Katz, 'Expanded Notions of Copyright Protection: Idea Protection within the Copyright Act' (1997) 70 Boston University Law Review, 883.

[67]Feldman, *op. cit.,* 696.

[68]Christian, 'Fan Fiction and the Fair Use Doctrine' (2013) 65(3-4) The Serials Librarian, 281.

with alternative characters, the characters can be used freely without reimbursing the author. Thus, some U.S. courts resort to what is known as the 'story being told' test[69] to determine whether a character is protectable or not, regardless of the elements of distinctiveness of such characters. For instance, in the *Sam Spade* case, the U.S. court concluded that the character concerned is uncopyrightable on the grounds that: firstly, the author had contracted with *Warner Bros.* to sell a specific series of *Falcon Sam*, and it was not indicated in the contract that the buyer will have exclusive rights upon the characters; secondly, *Falcon Sam* is only 'the chessman in the game of telling the story' and he is not a significant part of telling the story or a protagonist, thus, he is not protectable.[70] The court overlooked the interest of the public[71] and the influence of the character on the audience and its distinctiveness. It is difficult to find a character to be the nucleus of a story. Drawing from this case law, it can be fairly concluded that *Cinderella's* stepmother and step-sisters are not copyrightable.

Once a character is adequately established and, therefore, recognised outside of the film, such a character is likely to be afforded copyright protection[72] in both the U.K. and U.S. jurisdictions. For example, because *Harry Potter* is a distinguishable character outside of the film, the courts may prohibit other authors from exploiting such a character in their new fictitious works.[73] The court may consider many factors in deciding whether a character is distinctive and copyrightable namely: 1) the name of the character; 2) its visual appearance; and 3) the personality and attributes of such a character.[74] These elements are regarded as a yardstick to determine whether a character is recognisable outside the film.[75] Accordingly, characters that are not distinguishable

[69] *Warner Bro. Pictures, Inc. v. Columbia Broadcasting System, Inc.*, 216 F.2d 945 [1954].

[70] Ibid.

[71] Helfand, *op. cit.*, 633.

[72] Christian, *op. cit.*, 281.

[73] Ibid, 281.

[74] Ibid.

[75] Ibid.

after applying the aforementioned test are merely unprotected ideas of the author on the basis that they are not developed enough,[76] and any other author can create such simple and abstract characters. Thus, 'stock characters' cannot be protected.[77] In some U.S. cases, however, characters can be afforded copyright protection, despite the fact that they lack the aforementioned elements.

6. U.S. Overprotection of Fictional Characters

A number of U.S. decisions demonstrate the willingness of the court to side with copyrighted characters. This approach can be regarded as an expansion of copyright protection afforded to characters at the expense of the public domain.[78]For example, In *Warner Bros. v. X one X Productions*, the defendant used publicity materials depicting movie characters on a variety of products, such as t-shirts and lunch boxes.[79] It was held that reproducing pictorial materials featuring the characters was legitimate on the basis that they were in the public domain. However, the use of publicity images in model three-dimensional items infringed copyright on the grounds that it evoked someone's memory of the copyrightable aspects of the characters of the film more strongly than any single image. Although the concerned image was in the public domain, which meant that such image was eligible to be exploited in any way without the owner's authorisation, it infringed

[76]Ibid, 282.

[77]Schuster, 'Fair Use and Licensing of Derivative Fiction: A Discussion of Possible Latent Effects of the Commercialization of Fan Fiction' (2014) 55 South Texas Law Review, 537.

[78]Masnick, 'Wizard of Oz Court Ruling Suggests Moviemakers can Reclaim Parts of The Public Domain and Put it under Copyright'. (8 July 2011) <https://www.techdirt.com/articles/20110707/13110415001/wizard-oz-court-ruling-suggests-moviemakers-can-reclaim-parts-public-domain-put-it-under-copyright.shtml> accessed 12 April 2016.

[79]*Warner Bros. Entm't v. X One X Productions*, 10-1743 [2011] & Dowd

copyright law. This could make the public domain unreliable. Furthermore, it is difficult to imagine that an identical picture could be infringing copyrighted characters when it is in a 3-D form, and not infringing such characters when it is a normal flat image. Thus, mere modifications of the form of materials which are in the public domain may open the door to litigation on copyright infringement.[80]

In other U.S. cases, intangible elements of the character, such as thoughts, relationships, function and abstraction,[81] could be protected, although they are beyond the scope of copyright protection. For instance, in *Anderson v. Stallone*, the court concluded that an unauthorised sequel to the *Rocky* film based on the original characters constituted copyright infringement. The infringing action was subject to building on the relationships and experiences of *Rocky's* characters.[82] In this case, the subject matter of copyright was not based on protecting the characters individually and their appearance but, rather, protecting the characters collectively.[83] This could be regarded as an expansion of the protection of fictional characters, which also goes beyond the U.S. Term Extension of copyright protection.

7. U.S. Copyright Term Extension

According to the U.S. Copyright Act 1976, copyrighted characters created before 1976 would continue to be protected under copyright law for ninety-five years as a maximum, beginning from the date of dissemination.[84] Hence, *Mickey Mouse*, *Donald Duck, Goofy* and other well-known characters will pass into the public

---

80'Eighth Circuit: Adding a Phrase or Dimension to Public Domain Work is Copyright Infringement' (Copyright Litigation Blog, 6 July 211) < http://copyrightlitigation.blogspot.co.uk/2011/07/eighth-circuit-adding-phrase-or.html> accessed 12 April 2016.

81Ang, *op. cit.,* 116-117.

82*Anderson v. Stallone* 11 USPQ2D 1161 [1989].

83Schuster, *op. cit.,* 537.

84Liu,*op. cit.,* 1404.

domain in 2018.[85] For works completed after the adoption of the U.S. Copyright Act 1976 (i.e. after 1976), copyright would be valid as long as the author is alive, and for 70 years after the author's death.[86] This state of affairs was settled with an identified time period of exclusive commercial monopoly for authors, unless Congress extends the term of copyright again. [87] For example, *Mickey Mouse* was produced in 1928 and, under the U.S. Copyright Act 1909,[88] *Mickey's* copyright was supposed to expire and enter public domain in 1984.[89] Losing such an iconic character to the public domain would damage the Disney's Corporation's profits dramatically.[90] Courts usually extend the protection for such examples of expressive characters,[91] although a robust public domain, in all likelihood, is more significant than private interests.[92] The public domain attains society's advantage by providing a multitude of materials with which to create new works that benefit contemporary scholarship.

In the *Eldred* case, it was argued that extending the copyright duration of distinctive characters by using the Copyright Term Extension Act 1998 might violate the U.S. Constitution. The Constitution grants Congress the power 'to promote the progress of science and useful arts'.[93] Extensions which unduly exceed the life of a character's creator may not urge new creations and would impede many characters from entering the public domain, and

---

[85]Ibid.

[86]Ibid, 1400.

[87]Ibid.

[88]The term of protection was not more than 56 years. Helfand, *op. cit.,* 643.

[89]Crockett, 'How Mickey Mouse Evades the Public Domain' (Pricenomics, 7 January 2016) <http://priceonomics.com/how-mickey-mouse-evades-the-public-domain/> accessed 18 April 2016.

[90]Ibid Helfand, cited Kellman, *op. cit.,* 626-643.

[91]Helfand, *op. cit.,* 673.

[92]Crockett, *op. cit.*

[93]U.S. Constitution s 8.

then hinder building on them by the public.[94] Notably, copyrighted characters are mostly alienated from the authors to the eventual copyright owners.[95] Authors are usually under pressure to relinquish their copyright, and then its revenue, to those who invest in the dissemination of the authors' characters, such as film directors and film producers.[96] It is true that such transference occurs freely under contraction but, in fact, because of the market power of the commercial distributers, it is the only way to advertise such works to the wider public.[97] Thus, extensions are unlikely to motivate characters' creators, but they are likely to guarantee the profitability of film industry corporations. It was mentioned that extensions might provide an incentive to disseminate authors' works in the U.S.,[98] especially as the extensions are just for limited additional time periods, according to the Constitution.[99] Monopolising characters for a very long time could impede the development of new ideas based on such characters, for instance, the production of a film by someone other than Disney, for the purpose of reflecting regional problems, national costume or characterising municipal consuetude. Extensions to copyright protection are not derived solely from such U.S. terms, but also from derivative characters, as shown in the next part.

8. Derivative Works

Creators of expressive characters have exclusive rights to create and sell works which are derivative of their unexpired characters. They can adapt a character's semblance by changing some details. They can employ the character in new mediums rather than

[94]Reese, 'Is the Public Domain Permanent?: Congress's Power to Grant Exclusive Rights in Unpublished Public Domain Works' (2007) 30 Columbia Journal of Law & the Arts, 532-533.

[95]Jones, Lorenzen, & Sapsed, *The Oxford Handbook of Creative Industries* (Oxford: OUP 2015) 439.

[96]Ibid, 440.

[97]Ibid.

[98]Reese, *op. cit.,* 534.

[99]Ibid, 534. See also U.S. Constitution s 8.

films, such as in plays, or they can recast the character's personality and transform their shape.[100]In order to protect the derivative characters, new aspects should be added and only the new expressive aspects of such derivative characters will be protected, if the pre-existing (basic) characters have expired.[101]

Multiple versions based on creative characters may be created and published at different times.[102] This may make it more complex to distinguish between the expired elements of the character, which entered into the public domain and are available to everyone, and those new characteristics that are under copyright protection.[103] For instance, *Mickey Mouse's* portrayal has transformed over time. As long as the originality threshold in copyright is low, copyright may protect any new attachment to the character. Therefore, every version of Mickey is considered a derivative work.[104] This may restrict the use of expired works in the public domain rather than the new elements of derivative works. This facility could encourage authors to improve their characters when they are about to expire through adding unpretentious changes in order to extend the monopolistic period.

This situation is not uncommon in the U.S. For instance, in *Silverman v. CBS,*[105] the appellant, who was a musical scriptwriter, was charged with copyright infringement, under the 1909 Copyright Act, on the basis that the appellant's work was based on characters that originally appeared on the appellee's work. Although the characters were in the public domain, the court ruled that the appellant did not only employ the characteristics of the appellee's characters, which were in the public domain, but also used some idiosyncrasies of the character that were added later and existed in a copyrighted derivative work.[106] The issue is that the unprotected elements of the expired version of the character cannot be easily separated from the additional original

[100]Kellogg, *op. cit.,* 557.

[101]Helfand, *op. cit.,* 655.

[102]Liu, *op. cit.,* 1440.

[103]Ibid, 1441.

[104]Ibid.

[105]*Silverman v. CBS, Inc* 870 F.2d 40 [1989].

[106]Ibid.

elements,[107] and this may lead to protection of the whole character, including protection of the expired elements, which are supposed to be in the public domain. This situation has an impact on the credence of the works which are in the public domain.[108] In the U.K., derivative works will be protected if they differ significantly from the pre-existing work.[109] This difference may not be estimated according to the author's 'personal touch', but rather by the author's input of labour.[110] With this concern of maintaining copyright protection over fictional characters, freedom of speech could be confined.

9. Fictional Characters and Free Speech

U.S. copyright law is based on the idea that excluding other authors from using the protected characters encourages the production of creative fictional characters.[111] However, excessive control over fictional characters would raise free speech issues.[112] This excessive protection of fictional characters in the U.S., can lead to conflicts between proprietary characters and free speech. The owners of fictional characters would be indignant at the depiction of their characters in a displeasing manner, such as drinking alcohol or being used in a pornographic parody, even when the public knows that it is only a parody created by a third party.[113]

Employing fictional characters in parodies could present a method of amicable objection to demonstrate against oppressive regimes through joyful demolition.[114] People are using the charac-

[107]Liu, *op. cit.,* 1442.

[108]Ibid, 1444.

[109]Rahmatian, *op. cit.,* 26.

[110]Ibid, 26.

[111]Kellogg, *op. cit.,* 556 .

[112]Ibid, 558.

[113]Helfand, *op. cit.,* 628.

[114]Dery, 'Culture Jamming: Hacking, Slashing, and Sniping in the Empire of Signs' (2010) Scripted, 5.

ters to express their ideas and viewpoints.[115] These views may not be striking, but the use of well-known characters causes the statement to have an impact on the audience. It is difficult to imagine that a character's owner could penalise everyone who uses the character simply to criticise or to mock.[116] It was stated by commentators that characters' owners usually have the power to cease speech against their copyrighted properties even if the law permits such speech.[117] The cost of litigation is very high for individuals and that may suppress their freedom of speech.[118]

In *Walt Disney v. Air Pirates,* the court held that the defendant infringed copyright by using *Disney's* characters in comic books, even though parody may qualify for the fair use exception.[119] The court ruled that the defendant used the characters excessively and a parody should use them only to the extent of magnetising the audience to the subject matter of the mockery.[120] The court did not provide a conspicuous limit to using fictional characters. In *Elsmere Music v. National Broadcasting*, it was stated that, according to the substantial similarity test, the parody should only borrow the amount required to 'recall or conjure up' the copyrighted work.[121] Some commentators argue that the U.S. Court of Appeal provides a broad scope of protection to copyrighted charac-

---

[115]Egner, 'Intellectual Property-Trademark Law-Victor/Victoria?—The United States Supreme Court Requires Trademark Dilution Plaintiffs to Show Actual Harm. Moseley v. Victoria's Secret Catalogue, Inc., 537 U.S. 418 (2003)' (2004) 26 University of Arkansas at Little Rock Law Review, 318.

[116]Bunker, 'Mired in Confusion: Nominative Fair Use in Trademark Law and Freedom of Expression' (2015) 20(3) Communication Law and Policy, 195-196. This would be a device to silence speakers through the threat of an infringement lawsuit in every criticism or mocking.

[117]Rimmer, 'The Black Label: Trade Mark Dilution, Culture Jamming and the No Logo Movement' (2008) Scripted, 81 & 100.

[118]Ibid, 101.

[119]Helfand, *op. cit.*, 630.

[120]*Walt Disney Productions v. Air Pirates,* 581 F.2d 751 [1978].

[121]*Elsmere Music, Inc. V. National Broadcasting Co.* 482 F. Supp 741 [1980].

ters, which impinges on the First Amendment's guarantees of free speech.[122]

It is hard to find an academic article criticising famous characters, such as Hollywood or *Disney* characters. These characters may have a negative impact on a child's mental and psychological integrity. The criticism of characters such as *Scar* in *The Lion King* was to some extent timid. He was criticised for his violence, dark colour, and womanly mannerisms. These characteristics could encourage racism, homophobia or homosexuality.[123] Furthermore, personality, traits and attitudes in characters such as *Snow White*, *Ariel*, *Cinderella* and *Jasmine* could encourage and reinforce the idea that a woman is incomplete without a relationship with a man.[124] Criticism of characters depends on the public's concern to see a powerful corporation's characters being impaired and mocked,[125] in order to reinforce the traditional authority of religion, morality and humanity.[126]

10. Conclusion

Fictional characters are features that can make a spectator emotionally engage with a film.[127] It is common to hear an onlooker say that he feels miserable when a series of films come to an end because the characters had an influence on his life.[128] A spectator becomes inspired by the braveness of *Batman* and by the delicacy of *Cinderella*. These characters affect audiences deeply enough to compel them to buy tickets.[129] Protecting fictional char-

[122]Denicola, 'Copyright and Free Speech: Constitutional Limitations on the Protection of Expression' (1979) 67(2) California Law Review, 284.

[123]Kuwahara, *op. cit.,* 37.

[124]Hobbs & Rice, *Gender and Women's Studies in Canada: Critical Terrain* (Canada: Webcom 2013),337.

[125]Klein, *No Logo* (New York: Picador 2009) 287.

[126]Ibid, 287.

[127]Said, *op. cit.,* 770.

[128]Ibid, 771.

[129]Ibid, 772.

acters in films may be more important than other parts of the films, such as the dialogues, sound effects or methods of direction. This is because the characters have the ability to be completely separated from the original film[130] and be part of other films with different stories. They can also be used in commercials, and the images of them can be sold as part of items. Even theme parks were built based on these characters, such as *Disneyland*.

Characters are a significant part of the film industry. Fictional characters are considered to be the essential constituent of film marketing which leaves a special imprint on a film.[131] In the 1900s, U.S. courts struggled to conclude whether fictional characters are copyrightable. Nowadays, they are more willing to afford copyright protection to such characters. Fictional characters are often afforded copyright protection, which focuses on visual pictorial depictions more than characters that exist merely in literary works with a written description.[132] Such characters are considered as an expression in the copyright works, but they should be created independently. They should not be copied from others. A successful claim for copyright infringement is contingent upon the copyrightability and the originality of the fictional character.[133] Thus, characters should constitute a developed expression and not merely an abstract idea to gain protection.[134] '[T]he less developed the characters, the less they can be copyrighted; that is the penalty an author must bear for making them too indistinctly.'[135]

Many of the courts' decisions for the protection of fictional characters, through commercial monopoly, encourage authors to cover their ideas with attractive characters. Creators of distinctive characters deserve control over their work as a reward for their

---

[130]Ibid.

[131]Petridis, *op. cit.,* 286.

[132]Ibid, cited Nolan 281.

[133]Chatelain, *op. cit.,* 201.

[134]Bilsky, 'From Parts Unknown: WWE v. JIM Heewig in the Ultimate Battle for Character Copyright' (2009) 19(2). Marquette Sports Law Review., 429.

[135]Helfand, cited Judge Hand. *op. cit.,* 632.

intellectual ingenuity and cultural contributions.[136] Excluding others from reaping benefits from copyrighted characters emerging from the concept of moral rights is likely to establish copyright infringement. In the *Hill v. Whalen Mortell* case, a U.S. court concluded that the defendant's characters were similar to the plaintiff's characters and everyone viewing the former made an association with the latter.[137] It is not acceptable to ascribe creative characters to an infringer and it is unlawful to violate others' rights through unauthorised modifications or reproduction.[138] Such protection should not affect the doctrines of public domain, fair use and free speech.

There is some discrepancy between the U.S. perspective and the U.K. perspective in interpreting the common principles of protecting fictional characters under copyright law. There is also uncertainty and inconsistency in courts' decisions[139] in both the U.S. and U.K. jurisdictions. The threshold of the copyrightability of characters is too low, which may permit the granting of copyright protection to general characters, such as heroes or villains with no special visual appearance, traits or names.[140]

WORKS CITED

Primary Sources

Legislation

Copyright, Designs and Patents Act 1988.
Council Directive 93/83/EEC 1993

---

[136] Aplin, & Davis, *Intellectual Property Law: Text, Cases and Materials* (Oxford: OUF 2013), 51.

[137] Hill v. Whalen & Martell D.C.N.Y. 220 F. 359 [1914].

[138] Chung, 'Drawing Idea from Expression: Creation a Legal Space for Culturally Appropriated Literary Characters' (2007) 49(3) William and Mary Law Review, p 912.

[139] Schuster, *op. cit.,* 536.

[140] Bilsky, *op. cit.,* 429.

U.S. Copyright Act 1976
U.S. Constitution

Case Law

Anderson v. Stallone 11 USPQ2D 1161 [1989].
Bauman v. Fussell 1953 ca [1978].
Bezpečnostní Softwaro v. á Asociace C-393/09 [2010].
DC Comics v. Mark Towle, 802 F.3d 1012 9th Cir. [2015].
Detective Comics, Inc. v. Bruns Publications, Inc., 111 F.2d 432 2d Cir. [1940].
Elsmere Music, Inc. v. National Broadcasting Co. 482 F. Supp 741 [1980].
Feist Publications, Inc., v. Rural Telephone Service Co. 499 U.S. 340 [1991].
Football Association Premier League & Others v. QC Leisure & Others C-403/08 [2011].
Hill v. Whalen & Martell D.C.N.Y. 220 F. 359 [1914].
In Mattel, Inc. v. MCA Records, Inc, 296 F.3d 894 9th Cir. [2002].
Ladbroke Ltd v. William Hill 1 WLR 273 [1964].
Lucasfilm Ltd v Ainsworth EWCA Civ 1328 [2009].
Silverman v. CBS, Inc. 870 F.2d 40 [1989].
Walt Disney Productions v. Air Pirates 581 F.2d 751C.A.Cal. [1978].
University of London Press Ltd v. University Tutorial Press Ltd 2 Ch 601 [1916].
Warner Bro. Pictures, Inc. v. Columbia Broadcasting System, Inc., 216 F.2d 945 [1954].
Warner Bros. v. American Broadcasting 720 F.2d 231 [1983].

Secondary Sources

Books

Aplin T, and Davis, J. *Intellectual Property Law: Text, Cases and Materials* (Oxford: OUF, 2013).
Bently L, and Sherman, B. *Intellectual Property Law* (Oxford: OUP, 2014).

Hobbs M, and Rice, C. *Gender and Women's Studies in Canada: Critical Terrain* (Canada: Webcom, 2013).

Jones C,; Lorenzen, M.; & Sapsed, J. *The Oxford Handbook of Creative Industries* (Oxford: OUP, 2015).

Klein N, *No Logo* (New York: Picador, 2009).

Articles and Essays

Allan, R. 'After Bridgeman: Copyright, Museums and Public Domain Works of Art' (2007) 155(4) *University of Pennsylvania Law Review*, 961.

Ang, S. 'The Idea-Expression Dichotomy and Merger Doctrine in Copyright Laws of the U.S. and the U.K.' (1994) 2(2) *International Journal Law Information Technology*, 111.

Biswas, S. 'Copyrightability of Characters' (2004) 9 *Journal of Intellectual Property Rights*, 148.

Bunker, M. 'Mired in Confusion: Nominative Fair Use in Trademark Law and Freedom of Expression' (2015) 20(3) *Communication Law and Policy*, 195.

Chatelain, M. 'Harry Potter and the Prisoner of Copyright Law: Fan Fiction, Derivative Works, and the Fair Use Doctrine' (2012) 15 Tulane Journal of Technology and Intellectual Property, 199.

Christian, K. 'Fan Fiction and the Fair Use Doctrine' (2013) 65(3-4) *The Serials Librarian*, 277.

Chung, J. 'Drawing Idea from Expression: Creation a Legal Space for Culturally Appropriated Literary Characters' (2007) 49(3) *William and Mary Law Review*, 903.

Denicola, R. 'Copyright and Free Speech: Constitutional Limitations on the Protection of Expression' (1979) 67(2) *California Law Review*, 283.

Dery, M. 'Culture Jamming: Hacking, Slashing, and Sniping in the Empire of Signs' (2010) *Scripted.*

Egner, S. 'Intellectual Property-Trademark Law-Victor/Victoria?-The United States Supreme Court Requires Trademark Dilution Plaintiffs to Show Actual Harm'. *Moseley v. Victoria's Secret Catalogue, Inc.*, 537 U.S. 418 (2003)' (2004) 26 *University of Arkansas at Little Rock Law Review*, 303.

Feldman, D. 'Finding a Home for Fictional Characters: A Proposal for Change in Copyright Protection' (1990) 78 *California Law Review*, 687.

Helfand, M. 'When Mickey Mouse is as Strong as Superman: The Convergence of Intellectual Property Laws to Protect Fictional Literary and Pictorial Characters' (1992) 44 *Stanford Law Review*, 623.

Katz, J. 'Expanded Notions of Copyright Protection: Idea Protection within the Copyright Act' (1997) 70 *Boston University Law Review*, 873.

Kellogg, M. 'The Problem of Fictional Facts: Idea, Expression and Copyright's Balance between Author Incentive and Public Interest' (2011) 58 *Journal of the Copyright Society of the U.S.A.*, 549.

Kuhne, C. 'The Steadily Shrinking Public Domain: Inefficiencies of Existing Copyright Law in the Modern Technology Age' (2004) 50 *Loyola Law Review*, 549.

Kuwahara, Y. 'Japanese Culture and Popular Consciousness: Disney's The Lion King vs. Tezuka's Jungle Emperor' (1997) 31(1) *The Journal of Popular Culture*, 37.

Liu, J. 'The New Public Domain' (2013) 4 University of Illinois Law Review, 1395.

Madi, R. 'Mash-Up Songs: Are There Any Exceptions to the Exclusive Rights in the Light of the Jordanian Copyright Protection and Related Rights Law?' (2015) 18(3) *The Journal of World Intellectual Property*, 87.

Makulilo, A. 'Holy Copyright Law, Batman! The Batmobile is a copyright Character' (2016) 11(1) *Journal of Intellectual Property Law & Practice*, 12.

Petridis, S. 'Comparative Issues on Copyright Protection for Films in the U.S. and Greece' (2014) 19 *Journal of Intellectual Property Rights*, 282.

Rahmatian, A. 'Originality in U.K. Copyright Law: The Old "Skill and Labour" Doctrine under Pressure' (2013) 44(1) *International Review of Intellectual Property and Competition Law*, 4.

Reese, A. 'Is the Public Domain Permanent?: Congress's Power to Grant Exclusive Rights in Unpublished Public Domain Works' (2007) 30 *Columbia Journal of Law & the Arts*, 531.

Rimmer, M. 'The Black Label: Trade Mark Dilution, Culture Jamming and the No Logo Movement' (2008) *Scripted*, 70.

Said, Z. 'Fixing Copyright in Characters: Literary Perspectives on a Legal Problem' (2014) 35 *Cardozo Law Review*, 769.

Schuster, M. 'Fair Use and Licensing of Derivative Fiction: A Discussion of Possible Latent Effects of the Commercialization of Fan Fiction' (2014) 55 *South Texas Law Review*, 529.

Smith, M. 'The Limits of Copyright: Property, Parody and the Public Domain' (1993) 42(6) *Duke Law Journal*, 1233.

Internet Sources

'Western Animation / Mickey Mouse' (TV Tropes) <http://tvtropes.org/pmwiki/pmwiki.php/WesternAnimation/MickeyMouse?from=Main.MickeyMouse > accessed 9 April 2016.

Masnick, M.'Wizard of Oz Court Ruling Suggests Moviemakers can Reclaim Parts of The Public Domain and Put it under Copyright' (Techdirt, 8 July 2011) <https://www.techdirt.com/articles/20110707/13110415001/wizard-oz-court-ruling-suggests-moviemakers-can-reclaim-parts-public-domain-put-it-under-copyright.shtml> accessed 12 April 2016.

Dowd, R. 'Eighth Circuit: Adding a Phrase or Dimension to Public Domain Work is Copyright Infringement' (Copyright Litigation Blog, 6 July 2011) <http://copyrightlitigation.blogspot.co.uk/2011/07/eighth-circuit-adding-phrase-or.html> accessed 12 April. 2016.

Crockett Z. 'How Mickey Mouse Evades the Public Domain' (Priceonomics, 7 January 2016) < http://priceonomics.com/how-mickey-mouse-evades-the-public-domain/> accessed 18 April 2016.

International Competition Law: The Antitrust Damages Directive Feb 2016

Ruth Flaherty[1]

This article builds on previous works examining whether private enforcement should be prioritised over public enforcement for breaches of competition law within the EC. Data is analysed from European and national competition authorities case law, and from applicable explanatory documentation.

A new theory is laid out – that for the most efficient outcome both public and private enforcement should be utilised in different situations. Following the statement of intent in Preamble 6, Damages Directive 2014/104, 'both tools are required to interact to ensure maximum effectiveness of the competition rules'. This article uncovers that the Directive follows the direction of the European competition policy. Case law such as *Courage v Crehan*,[2] *Courage v Crehan*,[3] and *Kone*[4] demonstrate that private effects for damages should be at least as important as public enforcement strategies.

Other solutions–such as costs, proportionate damages, and collective redress–would be more effective than the current design, since the Directive arguably

[1]PhD Candidate, University of East Anglia Law School; Chair, Postgraduate Assembly, UEA Student Union.

[2]Case C-453/99 [2001] ECR I-6297.

[3]Case C-360/09 [2011] ECR I-5161.

[4]Case C-577/12 EU:C:2014:1317.

does not go far enough to incentivise private actions for damages.

Keywords: International Competition Law, Antitrust Damages Directive 2016, *Courage v Crehan, Kone, damages, private actions*

1. Introduction

The main objectives of the Damages Directive[5] are:

1. 'Optimising the interaction between the public and private enforcement of competition law; and
2. Ensuring that victims of infringements of the EU competition rules can obtain full compensation for the harm they have suffered'.[6]

There is an inherent tension between public and private enforcement, especially regarding its interaction with the leniency programme, as per Almunia:

> '...The Directive makes sure ... many cases that are likely to be heard in court will not encroach on the work of public enforcers. In particular, self-incriminating information released in the context of leniency programmes and settlement procedures will not be disclosed, and immunity recipients ... will be liable

[5]Directive 2014/104, hereinafter 'The Directive'.

[6]Commission, '*Antitrust: Commission proposal for Directive to facilitate damages claims by victims of antitrust violations – frequently asked questions*', 17 April 2014, <http://europa.eu/rapid/press-release_MEMO-14-310_en.htm> accessed 20/11/2016 , 2-3.

> only to their own customers and not to those of their co-cartelists'.[7]

Whilst there are many arguments for prioritising private or public enforcement,[8] this paper will propose that there should be a balance of the two; following the aim of the Directive that:

> "both tools (public and private enforcement) are required to interact to ensure maximum effectiveness *of the competition rules".[9]*

Towards this aim, this paper will argue that "the Directive comes out firmly in favour of safeguarding the effectiveness of public enforcement"[10], and it does not go far enough to incentivise private actions for damages; and by way of consequence, 'maximum effectiveness', as specified, has not been reached. To reach 'maximum effectiveness', there are other solutions available which could protect the aims of both private and public enforcement, overcoming the remaining enduring barriers to the effective recovery of damages – namely that of costs, and collective redress.

The following three tasks, of the enforcement of antitrust provisions, will be used as a guide to investigate what problems existed before the Directive, and to examine the provisions of the Directive in their light.

1. Clarifying and developing the law
2. Deterrence and punishment; and

---

[7]Almunia, J., European Commissioner Competition (2009-2014), 'Antitrust litigation – the way ahead' Speech to MLex Seminar, London 23 October 2014, < http://europa.eu/rapid/press-release_SPEECH-14-713_en.htm > accessed 20/11/2016.
[8]See for example Moeschel, W., '*Should Private Enforcement of Competition Law be Strengthened?*', GCLR 2013 6(1) 1-6.
[9]Preamble 6.
[10]Kwan, J., '*The Damages Directive*', ECLR 2015, 36(11), 455.

3. Corrective justice such as full compensation[11]

2. Historical background and rationale for the Directive

Prior to the implementation of the Directive, it was noted that victims of infringements of competition law only claimed compensation in 25% of all infringement decisions.[12] In comparison, in the US it was said that in one year alone more than 98% of cases were brought by private actors.[13] There was therefore an issue with under-utilisation of private enforcement mechanisms – arguably due to three issues which the Directive was designed to resolve: the historic centralisation of EC competition law; the lack of case law on the direct applicability of Articles 101 and 102 TFEU,[14] and that of access to evidence for claimants attempting to make a case.

2.1 The Historic Centralisation of EC Competition Law

Prior to the implementation of the Directive, only European authorities could enforce Articles 101 and 102. While this ensured that the rules were applied harmoniously, it led to a large adminis-

[11]Wils, W. P. J., *'The Relationship Between Public Antitrust Enforcement and Private Actions for Damages'*, World Competition 32(1) 2009, 5.

[12]In the years 2006-2013, Commission, 'Commission Proposes Legislation to Facilitate Damages Claims by Victims of Antitrust Violation', 11 June 2013, < http://europa.eu/rapid/press-release_IP-13-525_en.htm> accessed 20/11/2016.

[13]Odudu, O., '*Development of Private Enforcement in the EU'* [2008] 53 *Ant Bull* 873 (1150 cases out of 1165 in 2006-7).

[14]which contain the prohibitions regarding cartels and anti-competitive agreements, and abuse of a dominant position respectively.

trative burden being placed on the Commission, a backlog of cases forming,[15] and subsequent delays.

To act anti-competitively as a company is decided by the *individuals* working there, yet the *company* is punished by the imposition of fines or damages. Thus, when making this decision, the individuals weigh up the likelihood of personally being caught and punished. If individuals knew that even if the behaviour of the firm is flagged as anti-competitive, it is likely to be a long time before the case is brought before the Commission, it is likely to appear less of a deterrent – especially since it will give them a change to end the infringement or leave the company, which may provide them with a defence against personal claims.[16] Further, it's meant that the Commission's scarce resources were not used efficiently since they were investigating all cases, and thus couldn't focus on the largest or most complex cases.

2.2 The Lack of Case Law to Clarify and Develop the Law

Apart from the previous issue of a large administrative burden on the Commission, the Directive was also designed to provide a stronger restitutionary justice for private claimants[17] in order to balance private actions and public enforcement. This is despite the fact that prior to the Directive, Articles 101 and 102 TFEU had already been held to be directly applicable.[18] However, until 2001 there was no case in relation to national courts having a duty to provide private remedies. Consequently, this demonstrates an issue with using case law to clarify prohibitions – the consequent lack of clarity if no cases are brought on that topic, and this is important when the lack of clarity clearly disincentives private actions from being brought.

---

[15]By the end of 1998 this reached 1204 cases (EC Commission, *Twenty-Eighth Annual Report on Competition Policy 1998* (Brussels, 1999).

[16]D. I. Baker, 'Revisiting History – What Have We Learned About Private Antitrust Enforcement That We Would Recommend to Others?' (2004) 16(4) Loyola Consumer Law Review, 383.

[17]the ability to receive full compensation for their loss, Article 3(2).

[18]*BRT v SABAM* Case 127/73 [1974] ECR 51, 16.

While *Courage v Crehan*[19] "emphatically established a right to damages",[20]it is still left to the national courts to weigh up matters such as "the economic and legal context in which the parties find themselves";[21] which was followed by the case of *Manfredi*[22]. This flexibility, while allowing for arguments to be made on the facts in each case, led to a lack of coherence in case law across Europe which the Commission were trying to avoid. *Pfeiderer*[23] and *Kone*[24] extended this judicial support, for direct effect to damages caused by non-cartel companies, through 'umbrella pricing'; not only by helping private claimants move towards receiving full compensation, but also by creating an additional deterrence effect as highlighted that cases could be heard nationally, and by implication, quicker.

2.3 Access to Evidence for Claimants

In order for the law to act as a deterrent and to provide proper corrective justice, it must allow for cases to be brought to trial. Since cartels operate in the shadows, it is therefore hard for private claimants to make a case for infringement since they must prove that the defendants are guilty of infringing competition law and there is a causal link between that infringement and their loss.[25] Defendants will hold much of the evidence and will need a strong incentive to come forward; if they do not, infringing behaviour may not be discovered and punished, and so victims will not receive justice or compensation.

---

[19]Case C-453/99 [2001] ECR I-6297.

[20]Whish, R. and Bailey, D., Competition Law, (8th ed, 2015, OUP) 314.

[21]Ibid, 315.

[22]Cases C-295/04 *Vincenzo Manfredi v Lloyd Adriatico Assicurazioni SpA* [2006] ECR I-6619.

[23]Case C-360/09 [2011] ECR I-5161.

[24]*Kone AG v ÖBB-Infrastruktur* Case C-557/12 EU:C:2014:1317.

[25]Article 2 Regulation 1/2003.

Prior to the Directive, Regulation 1/2003 – the so called "linchpin of the modernised enforcement regime"[26] – tried to assist private claimants to overcome this by stating that once the Commission finds an infringement, it is binding on the national court in follow on actions, taking pressure off claimants *if* a public case has already been brought. As a consequence, this fails to assist with decreasing the burden on the Commission – since it implies the need for the prior case.

The Commission did not approach the barrier of access to evidence before the Directive, since the promotion of private actions came into direct competition with the leniency policy of the EC, "one of the most effective weapons against cartels".[27] This is an important meeting point, where incentivising private enforcement directly contradicts the incentives that the Commission have laid down for public enforcement.

2.4 Leniency

Leniency, based on the EC Leniency Notice,[28] has been called the "point of balance"[29] between private and public enforcement. Leniency on its own does not sufficiently meet the deterrence aim of competition law; it is ill equipped to deter cartels due to its lack of strong enough sanctions.[30] Plaintiffs want early and easy access to documents and easy proof of harm and causation, while defendants want to protect confidential business secrets and their self-incriminating leniency documents – to avoid becoming an easy target for damages claims through follow-on actions. The

---

[26]Jones A. & Sufrin, B., *EU Competition Law*, (5th ed, 2014, OUP), at 923.

[27]*Commission, 'Observations of the European Commission Pursuant to Article 15(3) of Regulation 1/2003, National Grid Electricity Transmission PLC', 3 November 2011, <http://ec.europa.eu/competition/court/amicus_curiae_2011_national_grid_en.pdf> accessed 20/11/2016.*

[28][2006] OJ C298/17.

[29]Migani, C., *'Directive 2014/104/EU'*, GAR 2014 Issue 14, 82.

[30]Stephan, A., *'An Empirical Assessment of the European Leniency Notice'*, 5 J. Competition L. & Econ. 537 (2009).

leniency system works upon the principle that it incentivises cartel members to be the first to notify the Commission (since only the first applicant receives full immunity); however, it has been argued that if the Commission's case is openly published, it may create the "First Mover Disadvantage"[31] whereby leniency applicants, who to save time and resources are likely to plead guilty (and not appeal), are the first targets for private actions for damages.

2.5 Disclosure of information from Leniency Applications

It was held in the cases of *Pfeiderer*[32] and *Donau Chemie*[33] that the decision whether to disclose the information, contained within a leniency application, should be decided on the facts of each individual case. This flexibility could act as a defence to the aim of justice as it allows for the question of disclosure to be raised in court; but, it has a strong negative effect on legal certainty, as the ECJ did not make it clear how disclosure should be decided.[34]

Thus, the national courts followed their own jurisprudence on disclosure of leniency information; and by way of example, Germany followed a "hard-line approach"[35] in *Roasted Coffee*[36]—whereby the interests of an effective leniency programme was held more important than the interests of victims, to bring private cases and receive compensation. The opposite ruling was made

---

[31]Böge, '*Leniency Programs and The Private Enforcement of European Competition Law'*, in Basedow (ed), *Private Enforcement of EC Competition Law*' (Alphen aan den Rijn, 2007), 221.

[32]See n 14.

[33]*Bundeswettbewehrbehörde v Donau Chemie AG* Case C-536/11.

[34]Kirst, P. and Van den Bergh, R., '*The European Directive on Damages Actions: A Missed Opportunity to Reconcile Compensation of Victims and Leniency Objectives'*, J. Competition L. & Econ., (December 2015) available at http://jcle.oxfordjournals.org/content/early/2015/12/08/joclec.nhv033.full , accessed 07/01/2016, 5.

[35]AG Bonn, Kein Zugangsrecht Kartellgeschädigter zu Kronzeugen unterlagen des BKartA, Jan 18, 2012 [NJW] 881.

[36]Oberlandesgericht [OLG], Aug 22, 2012, Case V-4 Kart 5 + 6/M (Owi).

in *National Grid,*[37] where the court held that immunity from fines was enough of an incentive for firms to partake in leniency actions; giving a clear need for further clarification, as allow for better access to justice for claimants since there was a clear divergence in cases within Europe.

3. How successful was the Directive in achieving its aims?

3.1 Leniency

The most important and successful change that the Directive made, towards incentivising private enforcement, was the extension of the limitation period for claimants to bring a claim to five years.[38] This brought more private claims within the purview of the court, since the five-year period begins when the claimant reasonably could be expected to be of the infringement,[39] identities at least one member of the alleged cartel, and that it caused the claimant harm. As mentioned, access to information such as the existence of the cartel and its membership were issues that previously curtailed the amount of private cases being brought, so these changes meant that even if claimants took time to find the information, they would not be prevented from bringing a case due to expired limitation periods (since it would not have begun to run before they had the information).

This largely benefits claimants when not only provides necessary time to create the claim, but also allows them to open up old claims for losses, which assists with the full compensation aspect of the Directive.

The change to limitation periods, within Article 10 of the Directive, also acts as a deterrent when it is potentially an additional cost for companies considering joining a cartel, since it is a liability that may apply at any indeterminate time. Due to the related

[37]*National Grid v ABB* [2012] EWHC 869 (Ch) 34.

[38]Article 10(5).

[39]Article 10(2).

rules on joint and several liability, it may also act as an incentive to act as a whistleblower if already infringing.

3.2 Joint and Several Liability

Joint and several liability[40] is designed partly to assist claimants claiming for compensation from any of the joint infringers. Although advantageous for the claimant, it seriously harms the defendant and therefore disincentivises them from claiming leniency. Further, is the risk that claimants may eventually lose out if the number of leniency applicants (and therefore the amount of information about cartels) falls.

Assisting further with balancing the needs of private and public enforcement, the Directive recognised the burdens it places on leniency applicants and SMEs: they could end up being liable for damages relating to the harm the full cartel caused, rather than just their share. Thus, the Directive clearly tried to balance out the rights of leniency applicants and SMEs through exceptions limiting their liability to purely their own direct or indirect customers – while at the same time leaving them liable as a last resort if claimants cannot claim full compensation from non-cooperating or larger defendants.[41]

3.3 Decisions of National Competition Authorities

The Directive also makes it easier for private claimants to sue (and therefore redresses the balance between public and private enforcement) by making it clear that decisions by national competition authorities can be used to prove fault in their own member state, and are at least prima facie evidence in other member states.[42] This improvement however is balanced out by the Directive, in "sharp contrast"[43] to previous case law such as *Pfeiderer*, stating that self-incriminating leniency documents were 'blacklist-

[40] Article 11(5).
[41] Article 11(2)-(4).
[42] Article 9.
[43] Kwan, J., 458.

ed'[44] from disclosure (rather than being a matter of fact for the court to decide whether it was reasonable to release the documents).[45] This was designed to protect public enforcement, which depends to a great extent on the success of leniency programmes, and so acted as a brake to some of the more claimant-friendly sections of the Directive. Still, this is an additional area where clarity is required, since an argument has been made that "the new Directive does not bring about any changes to the rules on access to documents"[46] due to the operation of ss 2-3 of Article 6, which curtail its effects. It remains to be seen how this will play out in actual cases.

3.4 Standing of Indirect Purchasers and the Passing on Defence

The final area where the Directive made changes was to create a-EU wide requirement, for recognising both the standing of indirect purchasers[47] and the passing on defence,[48] mainly to ensure that claimants are not overcompensated by recouping losses from several defendants in the same supply chain. This can be seen to assist private enforcement since it widens the pool of potential claimants who can bring a case. Still, whether this will always lead to an equitable outcome has yet to be argued.[49]

4. Issues that the Damages Directive Did Not Solve

Unfortunately, although the Directive specifically allows for all victims to claim full compensation,[50] it does not discuss the realistic

[44]Article 6(6).
[45]Article 6(1).
[46]Kirst, P and Van den Bergh, R., 10-11.
[47]Article 12(1).
[48]Article 13.
[49]Drexl, J., Gallego, B.C., Enchelmaier, S., Mackenrodt, M., Podszun, R., '*Comments of the Max Planck Institute*', IIC 2008, 39(7), 799-811.
[50]Article 3.

issue that blocks victims from claiming that of costs. This is a major barrier to the effective recovery of damages since competition law cases can be expensive to litigate, for example since cases require expensive analysis to prove economic harm and causation. Not only does the claimant have to bear the costs of their argument, but they "also carry the risk of having to pay the other side's costs if the claim is not made out", meaning that "there is little incentive to bring actions".[51] While a pan-member state cartel may have negatively affected many victims, the value of their individual harm may not be high enough to overcome the risk of litigating. In recognition of this, when bringing a case, the White Paper listed the potential deterrents as "costs, delays, uncertainties, risks and burdens".[52]

The Directive does not directly mention costs at all. The only way it attempts to reduce the cost burden for the claimant is through general methods of improving their position, such as those in Articles 9 and 17. Article 9 reduces the administrative burden on claimants by ensuring that if an action had been deemed to be anti-competitive by a national competition authority in another EU state, a claimant can rely on that decision rather than having to undertake their own costs to prove it. They must only prove therefore how the action negatively affected them. Article 17 reduces some of the burden for claimants since it makes it a rebuttable presumption that cartels cause harm. Thus, as in Article 9, this reduces some of the burden for the claimant and ensures the burden is on the defendant to prove that their actions did not cause the harm complained about.

It can therefore be said that the Damages Directive in this area does not strike the right balance between encouraging private actions for damages and protecting private enforcement, specifically because it does not mention costs and thus cannot be said to offer full corrective justice for victims, who may still be prevent-

---

[51]Holmes, K., *'Public Enforcement or Private Enforcement?'* ECLR 2004 25(1), 35.

[52]Commission, 'White Paper on Damages Actions for Breach of the EC antitrust rules', COM (2008) 165, 2 April 2008, <http://ec.europa.eu/competition/antitrust/actionsdamages/files_white_paper/whitepaper_en.pdf > accessed 20/11/2016, 4.

ed from bringing claims. If this happens, then it can also be said that the Directive is also failing to sufficiently punish anti-competitive behaviour.

5. Recommendations

The European Commission was incorrect in its belief that leniency incentives are incompatible with full compensation of victims, as demonstrated by Kirst and Van den Bergh[53] who propose that all immunity recipients receive immunity from not only fines but also damages (in the same proportions as given by the leniency application), and that this is extended to all undertakings who cooperate. This would answer the criticism of the Leniency process as it would give it more teeth as the benefit to cooperating undertakings would be larger (and any non-cooperating cartel members would be jointly and severally liable for the full damages caused without any possibility of being compensated). This solution "better optimises the interaction between public and private enforcement than the Directive is able to do"[54] and follows Almunia's argument[55] that immunity recipients should be protected.

However, the issue of costs would still stand, so I argue that while it should be implemented, a new enforcement mechanism should be introduced – that of a compensatory fund whereby private damages are integrated into public enforcement proceedings. Private damages that are estimated by the court alongside the fine and paid into a fund, which is then distributed by the court to injured parties, is a "consistent development of competition enforcement measures".[56] It aims to protect the interests of those bringing private damages actions, since it increases legal certainty and it too avoids the issues of access to evidence, since the

[53]Kirst and Van den Bergh, 17.

[54]Kirst and Van den Bergh, 19.

[55]Almunia, J., n 6.

[56]Canenbley, C and Steinvorth, T, '*Effective Enforcement of Competition Law*', J. *European Comp. Law & Practice* (2011), 2(4), 324.

private claimants wouldn't need to prove a factual case (i.e. the existence of the cartel), purely that they suffered harm as a result of the cartel.

Before the introduction of the Damages Directive, it appeared that the European Parliament was aware that "collective redress – with appropriate safeguards – is necessary".[57] The main reason for this is to promote the 'full compensation' function of the Directive, whereby all those harmed by anti-competitive actions are compensated for their loss. Although it was discussed in the Green Paper, it was dropped from the White Paper and the subsequent Directive, instead being raised in the accompanying Collective Redress Recommendation,[58] which is not legally binding. The UK has chosen to implement this in the Consumer Right Act 2015, but many countries have not. This due to the fact that 'appropriate safeguards' have not yet been met to avoid over litigation, the same reason that class actions are waning in popularity in the States (*AT&T Mobility LLC v Concepcion*[59] – and *Wal-Mart Stores, Inc, v Dukes*).[60] Thus, while this would improve the position with reference to costs, it may swing the pendulum too far towards claimants.

These recommendations would overcome the remaining barriers to the effective recovery of damages which endure beyond the application of the Directive,[61] but since they run counter to its provisions they are unlikely to be implemented in the short term.

---

[57]Press Release, '*Commissioner Kroes Welcomes the European Parliament's Cross Party Support for Damages for Consumer and Business Victims of Competition Breaches'*, Mar 26, 2009, available at http://europa.eu/rapid/press-release_MEMO-09-135_en.htm?locale=en , accessed 07/01/2016.

[58]C(2013) 3539/3, 11.6.2013.

[59]Case 09-893 (2011).

[60]Case 10-277 (2011).

[61]Such as collective redress and costs, as mentioned above.

6. Conclusion

This paper has shown that the Damages Directive was a step along a pre-existing path of jurisprudence in this area, and that while in some regards it encouraged private actions for damages while balancing the need for protecting public enforcement, the correct balance was not met. While it introduced the "very significant change" of joint and several liability[62] in Article 11, it did not go far enough to ensure full compensation of victims. Thus, although it makes improvements with regards to clarity and deterrence, it does not succeed in "providing compensation to achieve corrective justice"[63] as it is still too difficult for private actions to be brought, mostly due to the lack of movement on costs and collective redress. My recommendations are that proportionate damages are used and are integrated into the public enforcement to overcome these barriers.

Works Cited

Primary Sources

Legislation

Council Regulation (EC) No 1/2003/EC of 16 December 2002 on the implementation of the rules on competition laid down in Articles 81 and 82 of the Treaty [2003] OJ L1/1

Commission Notice on Immunity from Fines and Reduction of Fines in Cartel Cases (Leniency Notice) [2006] OJ C298/17

Commission Recommendation of 11 June 2013 on common principles for injunctive and compensatory collective redress mechanisms in the Member States concerning violations of rights granted under Union Law, OJ L 201

[62] Kirst, P and Van den Bergh, R., Ibid, 11.

[63] Wils, W.P.J, Ibid, 5.

Cases

Pfleiderer AG v Bundeskartellamt Case C-360/09 [2011] ECR I-5161
Vincenzo Manfredi v Lloyd Adriatico Assicurazioni SpA Cases C-295/04 [2006] ECR I-6619
Kone AG v ÖBB-Infrastruktur Case C-557/12 EU:C:2014:1317
Bundeswettbewehrbehörde v Donau Chemie AG Case C-536/11 ECLI:EU:C:2013:366
CDC Hydrogene Peroxide v Commission, Case T-437/08 [2012] 4 CMLR 14
EnBW v Commission, Case T-344/08 2012 OJ (C194)
Netherlands v Commission, Case T-380/08
BRT v SABAM Case 127/73 [1974] ECR 51, 16.
Courage v Crehan Case C-453/99 [2001] ECR I-6297
National Grid v ABB [2012] EWHC 869 (Ch) 34
Roasted Coffee Oberlandesgericht [OLG], Aug 22, 2012, Case V-4 Kart 5 + 6/M (Owi)
AT&T Mobility LLC v Concepcion Case 09-893 (2011)
Wal-Mart Stores, Inc, v Dukes Case 10-277 (2011)

Secondary Sources

Books

EC Commission, *Twenty-Eighth Annual Report on Competition Policy 1998* (Brussels, 1999)
Jones A and Sufrin B, *EU competition law: Text, cases, and materials* (5th edn, Oxford University Press 2014)
Whish R and Bailey D, *Competition law* (8th edn, Oxford University Press 2015)

Articles

Baker DI, 'Revisiting History – What Have We Learned About Private Antitrust Enforcement That We Would Recommend To Others?' (2004) 16(4) *Loyola Consumer Law Review* 379–408
Böge U, 'Leniency Programs and The Private Enforcement of European Competition Law' in Jurgen Basedow (ed), in *Private*

Enforcement of EC Competition Law (Kluwer Law International 2007) 217–228

Canenbley C and Steinvorth T, 'Effective enforcement of competition law: Is there a solution to the conflict between leniency programmes and private damages actions?' (2011) 2(4) *Journal of European Competition Law & Practice* 315–326

Drexl J and others, 'Comments of the Max Planck Institute for Intellectual Property, Competition And Tax Law on the White Paper by the Directorate General for Competition of April 2008 on damages actions for breach of the EC antitrust rules' (2008) 39(7) *International Review of Intellectual Property and Competition Law* 799–811

Foer AA and Schultz EP, 'Will Two roads still diverge? Private enforcement of antitrust law is getting harder in the United States. But Europe may be making it easier' [2011] (3) *Global Competition Litigation Review* 107–112

Holmes K, 'Public Enforcement or Private Enforcement? Enforcement of Competition Law in the EC and UK' (2004) 25(1) *European Competition Law Review* 25–36

Kirst P and Van den Bergh R, 'The European Directive on Damages Actions: A Missed Opportunity to Reconcile Compensation of Victims and Leniency Objectives' [2015] *Journal of Competition Law and Economics* 1–30

Kwan J, 'The Damages Directive: end of England's eminence?' (2015) 36(11) *European Competition Law Review* 455–462

Migani C, 'In search of a balance between the protection of leniency corporate statements and an effective private competition law enforcement' [2014] (4) *Global Antitrust Review* 81–111

Moeschel W, 'Should Private Enforcement of Competition Law be Strengthened?' (2013) 6(1) *Global Competition Law Review* 1–6

Odudu O, 'Developing Private Enforcement in the EU: Lessons from the Roberts Court' (2008) 53(4) *The Antitrust Bulletin* 873–902

Stephan A, 'An Empirical Assessment of the European Leniency Notice' (2008) 5(3) *Journal of Competition Law and Economics* 537–561

Wils WPJ, 'The relationship between public antitrust enforcement and private actions for damages by Wouter P. J. Wils: SSRN' (2009) 32(1) *World Competition* 3–26.

Press Releases and Speeches

Almunia, J., European Commissioner Competition (2009-2014), *'Antitrust litigation – the way ahead'* Speech to MLex Seminar, London 23 October 2014, < http://europa.eu/rapid/press-release_SPEECH-14-713_en.htm > accessed 20/11/2016

Commission, *'Antitrust: Commission proposal for Directive to facilitate damages claims by victims of antitrust violations – frequently asked questions',* 17 April 2014, <http://europa.eu/rapid/press-release_MEMO-14-310_en.htm> accessed 20/11/2016

Commission, '*Commission Proposes Legislation to Facilitate Damages Claims by Victims of Antitrust Violation*', 11 June 2013, < http://europa.eu/rapid/press-release_IP-13-525_en.htm> accessed 20/11/2016

Commission, '*Commissioner Kroes Welcomes the European Parliament's Cross Party Support for Damages for Consumer and Business Victims of Competition Breaches',* 26 March 2009, < http://europa.eu/rapid/press-release_MEMO-09-135_en.htm?locale=en > accessed 20/11/ 2016

Other

Bonn, A.G., *Kein Zugangsrecht Kartellgeschädigter zu Kronzeugen unterlagen des BKartA',* Jan 18, 2012 [NJW] 881

Commission, *'Observations of the European Commission Pursuant to Article 15(3) of Regulation 1/2003, National Grid Electricity Transmission PLC',* 3 November 2011, <http://ec.europa.eu/competition/court/amicus_curiae_2011_national_grid_en.pdf> accessed 20/11/2016

Commission, '*White Paper on Damages Actions for Breach of the EC antitrust rules',* COM (2008) 165, 2 April 2008, <http://ec.europa.eu/competition/antitrust/actionsdamages/files_white_paper/whitepaper_en.pdf > accessed 20/11/2016

Peyer S, 'Compensation and the damages directive' CCP Working Paper 15-10 <http://competitionpolicy.ac.uk/documents/

8158338/8368036/15-10+CCP+Working+Paper/
78f92b0e-6f92-4538-bca7-4f45e8de7b2b> accessed 16
November 2016 1–30

The Resounding Success of the Insurance Act 2015 with a Slight Blemish

Jiannan Lin[1]

Since the Insurance Act 2015 came into effect, it is meaningful for people in the Insurance Industry to be acquainted with certain key changes and/or some reasons of these changes. Official materials, such as Law Commission report relevant to Insurance Contract Law and oral or written evidences from the Bill Committee on Insurance Bill, are selected to deduce what ought to be the judicial practice. A certain amount of prejudication or case law is also of benefit to our perception of the Insurance Act 2015. These materials indicate that the Insurance Act 2015 balances various interests and is going to be impactful around the world. The article is divided into four main parts: the first is an introduction to the principles of fair presentation and proportionate remedy; the second is an analysis of breach of warranty in the context of the new Act; the third examines remedies for fraudulent claims; and the last part looks at how the Act is supplemented by the Enterprise Act 2016 on the issue of compensation of late payment.

Key Words: Insurance Act 2015, Enterprise Act 2016, duty of good faith, fair presentation, warranty, fraudulent claims, late payment.

---

[1]LLM, University of Exeter School of Law; Associate, EY Chen & Co Law Firm.

1. Introduction

It is common ground that insurance is inevitably indispensable to today's volatile commercial society, especially in maritime commerce. The Marine Insurance Act 1906 (the 1906 Act) was established in favour of the insurer in situations where the fledgling insurance industry was weak in getting information as a whole. The 1906 Act makes it easy for the insurer to make the contract null and void or to reject claims or to discharge their liability even in extreme cases, where there are only disproportionate nonfeasances of the assured. Now, a century later, the modern insurance system has turned assumptions of communication and data analysis inside out. In addition, not only small and medium-sized enterprises, but also big businesses, have insufficient skills and knowledge to realise all facts and demands which may be material in the eyes of insurers.[2] Even some brokers may not be aware of the severe or negative influences of the duty of utmost good faith.[3] Furthermore, negotiation power imbalances are evident between insurers and assureds, as insurers are likely to be the relatively high-power party during an insurance contract negotiation. Amongst the western legal systems, UK insurance law has already fallen into disfavour among many international assureds.[4] This is the reason why insurance law should be reformed, shifting from its insurer-favour position to an equilibrium pattern, although this codification may create a few further uncertainties.[5] The Insurance Act 2015 (the Act) draws some distinctions between con-

[2]Law Commission, 'Insurance Law Non-Disclosure and Breach of Warranty' (Law Com No 104, 1980).

[3]Law Commission, 'Insurance Contract Law: Business Disclosure; Warranties, Insurers' Remedies for Fraudulent Claims; and Late Payment' (Law Com No 353 2014).

[4]Law Commission, 'Insurance Contract Law: Misrepresentation, Non-Disclosure and Breach of Warranty by the insured' (Law Com CP No 182 2007).

[5]Robert Merkin, Colin Croly, 'Doubts about insurance codes' (2001) JBL 587.

sumers and businessmen.[6] Taking volunteer information, which applies to information not specifically asked for by the insurer on the proposal form, as an example, commercial assureds are still under a duty to volunteer information, while consumers are only bound to carefully and honestly answer questions.

This work largely aims at commercial insurance situations, as duties of consumer policyholders are governed by the Consumer Insurance (Disclosure and Representations) Act 2012. The reform of the Act mainly focuses on three areas. First, the duties of disclosure and misrepresentation have been superseded by the duty of "fair presentation". Some proportionate remedies are introduced when these duties are breached. Second, the "basis of the contract" clause has been abolished and breach of a warranty will no longer automatically discharge the liability of the insurer. Third, the Act provides the insurer with the statutory remedies for fraudulent claims. In addition, the section of damages for late payment was taken away from the insurance Bill, but supplemented by the Enterprise Act 2016. Accordingly, the structure of this work will mostly follow the four parts above.

2. The first reform: the duty of fair presentation

Non-disclosure and misrepresentation, as stated in the 1906 Act, have been replaced by the duty of fair presentation in the Act. Compared with "every material circumstance", that should be disclosed under the old law, "fair presentation" is a downscaled concept.[7] It means that the materiality test and the way of disclosure are redefined. The Act changes the state of the insurer from a passive recipient of information to the one taking the initiative in

[6]Law Commission, 'Insurance Contract Law: Misrepresentation, Non-Disclosure and Breach of Warranty by the insured'.

[7]Law commission, 'Insurance Contract Law: The Business Insured's Duty of Disclosure and the Law of Warranties' (Law Com CP No 204, 2012).

asking questions and indicating the information the insurer wants to learn.[8]

2.1 The related concepts

Some basic concepts should be mentioned as paving the way for a better understanding of the reform.

2.1.1 The duty of good faith

According to sections 14(1), (2) and (3)(b) of the Act, avoidance, which used to be the only remedy for the breach of the duty of good faith, has been replaced by proportionate approaches. This point will be further discussed below. Under the old law, a policy of insurance is governed by or based upon the principle of utmost good faith,[9] which is identified in the 1906 Act[10] and applies to all types of insurance.[11]

2.1.2 The difference between disclosure and representation

Before the Act, the assured's behaviour of non-disclosure and misrepresentation basically constituted a breach of the duty of utmost good faith.[12] There is a general difference between non-

---

[8]Law Commission, 'Insurance Contract Law: Business Disclosure; Warranties, Insurers' Remedies for Fraudulent Claims; and Late Payment'.

[9]Law Commission, Issues Paper 1, *Insurance Contract Law: Misrepresentation and Non-Disclosure* (2006) < http://lawcommission.justice.gov.uk/docs/ICL1_Misrepresentation_and_Non-disclosure.pdf > accessed 8 May 2015.

[10]Marine Insurance Act 1906, S 17, "A contract of marine insurance is a contract based upon the utmost good faith, and, if the utmost good faith be not observed by either party, the contract may be avoided by the other party."

[11]*Pan Atlantic Insurance Co Ltd v Pine Top Insurance Co Ltd* [1995] 1 AC 501.

[12]Susan Hodges, *Law of Marine Insurance* (Routledge-Cavendish, 1996).

disclosure and misrepresentation. The former focuses on the failure to disclose facts which are not mentioned in inquiry forms but which are material and known to the assured; whereas a misrepresentation occurs when the applicant fails to give true facts to specific questions in questionnaires, even if they are not aware that they made a misstatement.[13] In other words, a representation could be made out of "expectation or belief" which is beyond the scope of what the assured "knew or ought to have known".[14] The duty of disclosure in the old law is extremely stringent[15] and has been found to only support the insurer. The reason for this is that an innocent and honest assured may possibly be violating these kinds of obligation without realising the actual extent of these duties;[16] or even worse, they may know the duty but be uncertain of identifying which facts are material to a prudent insurer.[17] In any case, disclosure and representation are mainly acting on the basis of giving information just under different renderings; therefore, they could be replaced by a single concept such as "fair presentation". The Act aims at clarifying the duty of assureds to reveal material information. Section 3(3) of the Act establishes that the duty should be followed 'in a manner which would be reasonably clear and accessible to a prudent insurer'; the representation related to a matter of fact should be 'substantially correct'; and other representations should still be 'made in good faith'.[18]

13

Zurich General Accident and Liability Insurance Co v Leven 1940 S C 406.

14S 20 Marine Insurance Act 1906.

15Law Commission, 'Insurance Law Non-Disclosure and Breach of Warranty'.

16*Lambert v Cooperative Insurance Society Ltd* [1957] 2 Lloyd's Rep 485.

17Law Commission, *Consumer Insurance Law: pre-contract disclosure and misrepresentation* (Law Com No 319, 2009).

18ss 3(3) Insurance Act 2015.

2.1.3 The timing issue

The duty of fair presentation, which only exists before the conclusion of the insurance contract, is directed towards the assured.[19] No change has been made in this field. In the old law, *The Litsion Pride*[20] extended the liability of disclosure to the post-contract phase. However, Lord Jauncey held a distinct view in *Banque Keyser v Skandia*[21] that the assured was under no obligation to report facts that took place after the conclusion of the contract.[22] Furthermore, any misstatement given after the establishment of the insurance contract could not be seen as a representation in a legal sense.[23] So, generally speaking, the duty to disclose only exists before the insurance contract is formed or a variation occurs. In *Carter v Boehm*[24], Lord Ellenborough stated that the duty of utmost good faith is bilateral and reciprocal. However, His Lordship further stated that this duty actually heavily falls on the assured. This situation is also reflected in Section 20(1) of 1906 Act. If the policy is renewed, the duty of fair presentation should apply again. This provision keeps pace with the old laws.[25]

In conclusion, the duties of disclosure and representation have merged into a single duty of fair presentation. The time of performing the duty remains the same, but the consequence of breaching the duty has changed from an avoidance remedy to a proportionate remedy and the materiality test as the key of the duty is restated in the Act.

---

[19]S 3(1) Insurance Act 2015.

[20][1985] 1 Lloyd's Rep 437.

[21][1990] 2 Lloyd's Rep 377.

[22]*Iron Trades Mutual insurance Co v Companhia de Seguros Imperio* [1992] 1 Re. L. R. 213. Hobhouse J. held the same view.

[23]*Ionides v Pacific Fire & Mar Ins Co* (1891) L. R. 6 Q. B. 674.

[24](1766) 3 Burr 1905, 1 Wm Bl 593.

[25]Explanatory Notes to the Insurance Bill 2015.

2.2 The Restatement of the Materiality Test

In the pre-fair-presentation era, in light of Section 18(2) and 20(2) of the 1906 Act,[26] if non-disclosure or misrepresentation would influence a reasonable insurer's decision about the level of the premium or on whether to accept the risk, the insurer would stand in the position of avoiding the contract regardless of whether the non-disclosure or misrepresentation is relevant to the risks or not.[27] The interpretation of Section 20(2) of the 1906 Act varied several times. Under *C.T.I. Inc v Oceanus*,[28] material facts are matters by which a prudent underwriter would be attracted to launch an enquiry for more information before decision-making. Several years later, the test of materiality was adjusted by Lord Justice Steyn in *Pan Atlantic v Pine Top*.[29] That case held that if undisclosed facts were unwrapped, these material facts would be considered by a prudent underwriter as aggravation of risks. However, as mentioned above, the old test of materiality may be interpreted as the onerous task of requiring vast quantities of information without limitation. The duty of fair presentation, as the substitute of the duty of disclosure and representation, is not expected to make dramatic changes but to continue inheriting positive impacts from the current case law, which are not mentioned in the 1906 Act. These impacts include the inducement test and the insurer's waiver of information.

---

[26]Marine Insurance Act 1906, S18(2) "[e]very circumstance is material which would influence the judgement of a prudent insurer in fixing the premium, or determining whether he will take the risk." and S20(2) "[a] representation is material which would influence the judgment of a prudent insurer in fixing the premium, or determining whether he will take the risk."

[27]*Pan Atlantic Insurance Co Ltd v Pine Top Insurance Co Ltd* [1995] 1 AC 501. At page 527, Steyn LJ was quoted as stating that "avoidance for non-disclosure is the remedy provided by law because the risk presented is different from the true risk."

[28][1984] 1 Lloyd's Rep 476.

[29][1995] 1 AC 501.

2.2.1 The inducement test

The test for inducement was firstly introduced to further amend the test of materiality in *St Paul Fire and Marine Insurance Co Ltd v McConnell Dowell Constructors Ltd.*[30] Lord Justice Evans held the view that

> it was common ground that the insurer had to prove that he was induced by the non-disclosure or misrepresentation to enter into a contract on terms which he would not have accepted if all the material facts had been known to him.[31]

In other words, the insurer has been induced to conclude an insurance contract or agree with some special terms, due to undisclosed facts. These facts are deemed material. The essence of this leading case is mainly absorbed by the new test of materiality in the Act. Section 7(3) of the Act repeats the old law, that whether a fact is material depends on whether these facts will influence a prudent insurer to accept the risk or change the terms. Section 7(5) of the Act illustrates the criterion of substantial correctness of a material representation. It will make no difference in a prudent insurer's mind after he hears the full story. This is just a different saying of the inducement test. However, it could be argued that this test primarily depends on a crucial fact rather than a virtual situation where something else happens. In a motor insurance case,[32] two material facts were not disclosed. One was the assured's speeding conviction while the other was that the previous reported accident actually was a "no fault" accident. It was argued by the assured that if the speeding conviction had been disclosed, a higher premium would be charged; it presumably follows that the nature of the earlier accident might be corrected by the assured for returning the level of premium to normal. However, the judge stated that

---

[30][1995] 2 Lloyd's Rep 116.

[31]Ibid, 117.

[32]*Drake Insurance plc v Provident Insurance plc* [2003] EWCA Civ 1834.

> one simply does not know what [the assured]'s reaction to an increase in premium would have been. He might have questioned it, or he might not...There is nothing in the evidence that points either way. Only if it could be shown that disclosure of the conviction would also have led to the disclosure of the information relating the settlement of the earlier loss and to [the insurer] accepting the risk on the same terms could one say that the non-disclosure had not caused it to accept the risk on terms that it would not otherwise have agreed to.[33]

In conclusion, although the inducement test is not mentioned expressly in the Act, it has already been an integral part of the test of materiality in the Act.[34]

2.2.2 Sufficient information draw the insurer's attention to make an inquiring reaction

According to Section 3(4)(b) of the Act, a fair presentation should be deemed completed if disclosed information from the assured is sufficient for a prudent insurer to make a further inquiry to know more, and this test is objective.[35] Historically, according to Section 18(3)(c) of the 1906 Act[36], the insurer's lack of inquiry may sometimes constitute a waiver of information. It is argued by *MacGillivray on Insurance Law*[37] that if some information, which would arouse a prudent insurer's vigilance to know more about it, has been reported by the assured, and if the insurer is found negligent

---

[33]Ibid, para 28.

[34]Law commission, 'Insurance Contract Law: The Business Insured's Duty of Disclosure and the Law of Warranties'.

[35]Law Commission, 'Insurance Contract Law: Business Disclosure; Warranties, Insurers' Remedies for Fraudulent Claims; and Late Payment' .

[36]S18(3)(c) Marine Insurance Act 1906, "In the absence of inquiry the following circumstances need not be disclosed, namely: any circumstance as to which information is waived by the insurer."

[37]John Birds, Ben Lynch, Simon Milnes, *MacGillivray on Insurance Law* (12th edn, Sweet & Maxwell, 2012).

in further inquiries, the omission of the insurer will be held as a waiver for non-disclosure. This view was supported by Lord Justice Rix in *Wise Ltd. v. Grupo Nacional Provincial S.A.*[38] In that case, a Mexican insurance company (GNP) entered into a reinsurance contract (the slip form) with reinsurers (Wise) to cover the transit risk of a series of valuables. The stolen items included some expensive Rolex watches which were listed as "clocks" due to a translation mistake in the slip; however, it was clearly stated on the insurance slip that the insured subjects were "Clocks: less expensive piece: U.S. $40. Most expensive piece U.S. $18,000 and average cost U.S. $1,500."[39] This mistake was deemed as non-disclosure by the High court and the Court of Appeal. However, Lord Justice Rix considered that (1) the statement that the highest value of a clock reached up to U.S. $18,000 was enough to be regarded as "utterly unbusinesslike"[40]; (2) the duty of good faith should fall on both parties; (3) it was unfair that the insurer might know the problem about the insured subject matter, but can choose to "[keep] that information to himself"[41] without a simple or obvious question. His Lordship finally concluded that a waiver for non-disclosure was established. However, Lord Justice Longmore and Peter Gibson disagreed with Lord Justice Rix on the ground that "the assured cannot assert that if only the underwriter had asked an obvious question he would have discovered something which should have been disclosed."[42]

Their thoughts strictly reflected the rigid passivism of the 1906 Act, which has had a negative influence on the UK insurance market. The Mactavish Protocols report[43] makes it clear that the old pattern has actually been aggravating the UK insurance soft

---

[38][2004] 2 Lloyd's Rep. 483.

[39]Ibid, 487.

[40]Ibid, 500.

[41]Ibid.

[42]Ibid.

[43]Mactavish, 'Corporate risk & insurance the case for placement reform' (the Mactavish Protocals, 2011) http://www.airmic.com/system/files/Corporate%20Risk%20-%20Placement%20Reform%20EXECUTIVE%20SUMMARY.pdf accessed 28 June 2015.

market situations, decreasing policy dependability and certainty; an insurance company may pay less insurance compensation once in a while, but trust in UK insurance companies as a whole may be gradually eroded. Section 3(4)(b) of the Act clearly endorses the view of Lord Justice Rix. This test admirably meets the need to limit the duty of disclosure.

2.3 New concept of material circumstances

In addition to the above-mentioned point, material circumstances mentioned in Section 7(4) of the Act should also be disclosed. The first is special and unusual facts in relation to the risk. The "special and unusual fact" is a brand-new concept which was not mentioned in the 1906 Act but existed in common law. In *CTI*, Lord Justice Kerr stated that "[t]he doctrine of waiver cannot be applied to undisclosed facts which are unusual or special".[44] The second is that specific information particular to the class of insurance should be disclosed. However, what is uncertain is whether past losses are included in material circumstances. It might be argued that past losses related to the specific type of risk should be disclosed without the trigger of an inquiry, one reason being that past losses are usually regarded as unusual facts and should be included in a fair presentation of risk in Section 7(4)(c) of the Act;[45] the second reason is that the insurer is not in a position to know this kind of facts, so a waiver of information could not be formed.

2.4 Remedy of breach

When the duty of utmost good faith is breached under the old law, avoidance is the only remedy. Additionally, there is no need to es-

---

[44][1984] 1 Lloyd's Rep. 476, 498.

[45]*Mar Rich & Co v Portman* [1997] 1 Lloyd's Rep 225. In this case, the insurers take the risk without any questions, although the assured is expected to be asked about the previous loss. The court held that the presentation is unfair due to the silence of material facts of the loss which the assured is bound to know.

tablish a causation between the breach and the loss.[46] Before the Act, a right of compensation for damage is not available for breach of duty of utmost good faith.[47] A fierce critique of this "all or nothing" rule is contained in the Law Commission's 2007 Consultation Paper.[48] The reasons for supporting a proportional relief rule instead are that:

1. A proportionate remedy rule has been established in other legal systems. For example, in French Insurance Law, when a misrepresentation issue appears after a loss has happened, proportional relief is adopted.[49]
2. The old law loses sight of the mutual demand that the insurer might be willing to accept a remedial measure of breach of utmost good faith from the assured:[50] for example, a "held covered" clause is now widely used in marine policies.[51]

---

[46] *Seaman v Fonereau* (1743) 2 Stra 1183.

[47] Law Commission, 'Consumer Insurance Law: pre-contract disclosure and misrepresentation'.

[48] Law Commission, 'Insurance Contract Law: Misrepresentation, Non-Disclosure and Breach of Warranty by the insured'

[49] Law Commission, Issues Paper 1, 'Insurance Contract Law: Misrepresentation and Non-Disclosure (2006)' < http://lawcommission.justice.gov.uk/docs/ICL1_Misrepresentation_and_Non-disclosure.pdf > accessed 8 May 2015

[50] Ibid.

[51] The function of a "held covered" clause is to provide the assured by the insurer with one more chance to correct inadvertent breach of utmost good faith. In *Hewitt Brothers v Wilson.* [1915] 2 K.B. 739, a "held covered" clause was included in a marine policy which covered normal marine perils including risk of breakage. The insurer denied the insurance claim on the ground that there has been non-disclosure of the nature of machinery, due to the fact that one of the damaged machines caused by breakage is second-hand and was unmarked. Lord Reading C.J. at first explained that second-hand machines is quite a few parts of all machinery and the same policy has been continued many times and the insurer never asked for the class of machinery as other underwriters do. He finally held that the assured is protected by the "held covered" clause in the policy.

Moreover, the assured is more likely to conceal material information under the threat of avoidance.

3. A number of courts are reluctant to adopt this unfair and overly harsh remedy and find reasons in favour of the assured to gain full indemnity.[52] There is still another point that deserves attention: that it is difficult for proportionate remedy to perform well and quickly in a liability insurance situation, due to the burden of increasing cost and workload on the insurer.[53]

In general, the proportionate remedy is a creative and innovate measure for the benefit of the UK insurance market. The reform in fair presentation successfully and clearly restates prevalent and appropriate legal practices. However, the duty of fair presentation is nevertheless open to some doubt, which is discussed below.

2.5 Some uncertainties related to the assured's knowledge

2.5.1 Reasonable search

The Act requires the assured to undertake a "reasonable search" for knowledge available for "the insured's organization or any other person",[54] such as the covered parties and the broker. However, the Lloyd's Market Association ("LMA") and the International Underwriting Association ("IUA") believe that the reasonable search test is so board and vague that it is likely to lead to new tangles.[55] This test presents a challenging burden of proof to the

[52]Law commission, 'Insurance Contract Law: The Business Insured's Duty of Disclosure and the Law of Warranties'.

[53]Oral Evidence taken before the special public bill committee on Insurance bill (24 December 2014), Q 16, < http://www.publications.parliament.uk/pa/ld201415/ldselect/ldinsur/81/81.pdf > HL Paper 81, accessed 9 May 2015.

[54]S 4(6) and 4(7) Insurance Act 2015.

[55]Written Evidence taken before the special public bill committee on Insurance bill (24 December 2014), 'Written submissions of the LMA and IUA', < http://www.publications.parliament.uk/pa/ld201415/ldselect/ldinsur/81/81.pdf > HL Paper 81, accessed 9 May 2015.

insured and increases costs of factual and expert exploration, due to the fact that this test is based on an objective measure.[56] For example, some small companies may lack the resources to carry out a reasonable search as other middle-sized or big companies do; should the duty be interpreted too strictly, small companies would be punished in spite of having prudently executed research.[57] Furthermore, the duty of reasonable search, as a brand new legal rule, lacks support from the common law. However, it is also an opportunity to build a new business culture, such as operate procedures and record-keeping habits, and legislative context, which will be defined by the judiciary in light of the practice. According to Section 4(4) of the Act, insurance brokers are no longer under the duty stated in Section 19 of the 1906 Act[58] to reveal confidential information to the insurer. This may introduce a new uncertainty, such as whether the scope of the assured's reasonable search should reach the information intentionally concealed by the broker, like in *Proudfoot v Montefiore*.[59] In other words, it seems that the Act encourages the broker to hide information from the assured.

2.5.2 Senior management

The definition of "senior management" in Section 4(3) of the Act may also cause a slight uncertainty. Especially in a large multinational enterprise, a junior employee not involved with the insurance may be more probable to get hold of material information. In

---

[56]Ibid.

[57]Ibid.

[58]S 19 Marine Insurance Act 1906, "Disclosure by agent effecting insurance. Subject to the provisions of the preceding section as to circumstances which need not be disclosed, where an insurance is effected for the assured by an agent, the agent must disclose to the insurer—(a) Every material circumstance which is known to himself, and an agent to insure is deemed to know every circumstance which in the ordinary course of business ought to be known by, or to have been communicated to, him; and(b) Every material circumstance which the assured is bound to disclose, unless it come to his knowledge too late to communicate it to the agent."

[59](1867) LR 2 QB 511.

this situation, whether this junior manager is the one responsible for revealing material information is up to clarification by the courts.

In conclusion, the design of fair presentation is progressive and sets up an impartial and balanced mechanism for co-operation among the assured, the insurer and the broker. More importantly, it makes clear all participants' duties and rights referring to the exchange of information in order to establish the foundation of the rest of the reforms.

3. The second reform: warranty

The warranty is always essential to traditional English insurance law, but its scope and the consequences of its breach sometimes confused the participants in the old law. Therefore, a relevant reform is necessary. However, some parts of the warranty reform are startling changes, and as a result some new uncertainties are still pending for clarification through new judicial precedents and legislation consecutively.

3.1 The concept

A warranty is defined in Section 33(1) of the 1906 Act[60] and applies to other kinds of insurance with the common law growth. For the purpose of defining the risk, a warranty aims at keeping the assured's precautions, adding a remedy for the insurer, and laying the obligations on the assured to state the past existence, or to fulfil some conditions, or to keep the promise to do or not to do

[60] S 33(1) Marine Insurance Act 1906, "A warranty, in the following sections relating to warranties, means a promissory warranty, that is to say, a warranty by which the assured undertakes that some particular thing shall or shall not be done, or that some condition shall be fulfilled, or whereby he affirms or negatives the existence of a particular state of facts."

something.[61] The Act does not intend to change the definition of warranty.[62] Non-compliance with a warranty is not excusable in law unless:

1. the warranty is no more applicable due to circumstance alternation; or
2. is against the change of law; or
3. the insurer waives the warranty.[63]

However, these exceptions are insufficient to balance the situation, which is overwhelmingly in favour of the insurer by comparison to other common law jurisdictions.[64]

3.2 The reasons for the reform

The warranty in old insurance law has been criticized for several reasons. First, liabilities of the insurer can be wholly excluded, despite whether the breach only touches small part, or even no part, of the insured subject.[65] Additionally, the assured could breach a warranty even when he has no fault at all, and the insurer could still discharge from all further responsibilities, regardless of any causative connection between loss and breach of war-

---

[61]Law Commission, Issues Paper 2, *Insurance Contract Law: Warranties* (2006) <http://lawcommission.justice.gov.uk/docs/ICL2_Warranties.pdf> accessed 8 May 2015> accessed 8 May 2015.

[62]Explanatory Notes to the Insurance Bill 2015.

[63]S 34 Marine Insurance Act 1906.

[64]Law Commission, 'Insurance Contract Law: Business Disclosure; Warranties, Insurers's Remedies for Fraudulent Claims; and Late Payment'

[65]Jonathan Gilman, Robert Merkin, Claire Blanchard, Mark Templeman, *Arnould's law of marine insurance and average* (18th edn, Sweet & Maxwell, 2013) Chapter 19 Section 10. See also *Overseas Commodities Ltd v Style* [1958] 1 Lloyd's Rep. 546. In this case, a good deal of the insured objects (tins) did not conform to the warranty of the date-marking requirement, so the insurer is discharged from liability of the policies.

ranty.[66] As a result, the insurance warranty was widely regarded as a technical defence.[67] The meeting requirement of the duty of a warranty is more severe than that of non-disclosure and misrepresentation. When contract items or actions are mildly deficient according to the description of a warranty, the insurer could automatically get rid of all liability even though these unconformities were not considered important by both the prudent insurer and the actual insurer.[68]

Second, warranties could be easily and widely created.[69] Take "basis of the contract" clauses for example: a prospective assured has to answer a series of questions in an application form at the end of which an applicant has to sign a statement that "I declare that the particulars and statements made by me above are true, and I agree that they shall be the basis of the contract".[70] The effect of these words is to transform all statements of the assured into warranties, although statements may not be shown in the policy.[71] In addition, a warranty could also be established by assessing the common intention of parties in the court's discretion.[72] Any statements related to facts bearing upon the risk are equivalent to warranties and should be strictly observed.[73] In the understanding of the authors of *Arnould*,[74] facts bearing upon the risk amount to

[66]S 33(3) Marine Insurance Act 1906.

[67]John Hare, 'The Omnipotent Warranty: England v The World' in Marc Huybrechts and others (eds), *Marine Insurance at the Turn of the Millennium* (Intersentia, 1999).

[68]Law Commission, Issues Paper 2, 'Insurance Contract Law: Warranties' (2006) <http://lawcommission.justice.gov.uk/docs/ICL2_Warranties.pdf> accessed 8 May 2015> accessed 8 May 2015

[69]*Genesis Housing Association Ltd v Liberty Syndicate Management Ltd* [2013] EWCA Civ 1173.

[70]*Provincial Insurance Co. v. Morgan* [1933] A.C. 240, 251.

[71]R. A. Hasson, 'the "basis of the Contract Clause" in insurance law' (1971) 34(1) MLR 29.

[72]Baris Soyer, *Warranties in Marine Insurance* (2nd edn, Cavendish, 2006).

[73]*Thomson v Weems* (1884) 9 App. Cas. 671.

[74]Jonathan Gilman, Robert Merkin, Claire Blanchard, Mark Templeman, *Arnould's law of marine insurance and average* (18th ed, Sweet & Maxwell, 2013)

facts involving the insured subject matter in the policy. In summary, a warranty needs no specific form; this is why the assured may be unconscious of their existence until a loss has arisen.

Third, there is no visible solution for the assured to defend a breach of warranty even if the breach has been remedied before losses occur. For example, in *De Hahn v Hartley*[75], the words "[s]ailed from Liverpool with 14 six-pounders, swivels, small arms, and 50 hands or upwards; copper-sheathed" handwritten in the margin of a marine policy was considered as a warranty. The insured vessel with only 46 seamen sailed from Liverpool to Beaumaris to pick up other six seamen during the voyage. So the breach of warranty was established, but the breach was subsequently remedied after six hours. However, the judge avoided the responsibility of the insurer under the said policy due to the fact that the warranty was not complied with.

The concept of warranty has been chronically abused by the insurer,[76] and is in mismatch with general contract law; as a result, the warranty system is full of contradictions.[77] On one hand, the courts insist on rigorous performance of the principle of exact compliance of the warranty; on the other hand, warranties have been interpreted narrowly to protect the assured from harsh results in recent case law. For example:

1. in *Hussain v Brown*, the Court believed that a warranty does not apply to future facts;[78]

[75](1786) I Term Rep 343, 343.

[76]Rob Merkin, 'Reforming Insurance Law: Is there a case for reverse transportation?' < http://lawcommission.justice.gov.uk/docs/ICL_Merkin_report.pdf> accessed 4 May 2015.

[77]Carl Christian Rösiö, 'Warranties in marine insurance: an unpleasant necessity?' (Juridisk Publikation, 2010) < http://juridiskpublikation.se/wp-content/uploads/2014/10/12010_Carl-Christian-R%C3%B6si%C3%B6.pdf> accessed 4 May 2015.

[78]*Hussain v Brown* [2001] 2 Lloyd's Rep 161. The rule of warranty does not require a promise to continue into the further. A warranty that the premises were secured by an alarm should by no means be considered as a promise that an alarm would always be available in the future.

2. in *Printpak v AGF*, it was held that a warranty established in a type of risk should not extend to apply to other part of risks, when the insurance contract separately covers different risks;[79]

3. in *Houghton v Trafalgar Insurance Co Ltd*, it was pointed out that a warranty should not apply to the vague words in the "basis of the contract" clause;[80]

4. in an opinion by Michael Parkington and Nicholas Legh Jones, it was argued that although a promise is described in the way of "it is warranted that...", the clause still could be interpreted as a suspensive condition on the base of a purposive interpretation, which means that the breach had only been suspending the underwriting risk until the promise was kept.[81]

In *Kler Knitwear Ltd v Lombard General Insurance Company Ltd*,[82] the insurance policy contained the provision that

> [i]t is warranted that within 30 days of renewal 1998 the sprinkler installations at the Jellicoe Rd/Gough Rd/ Spalding Rd locations must be inspected by a LPC approved sprinkler engineer with all necessary rectification work commissioned within 14 days of the inspection report being received.[83]

However, the fact was that the sprinkler installations were not inspected until up to 60 days after the time limit, and the sprinkler installations were good according to the inspection report. Justice Morland regarded the provision as a suspensive condition instead of a warranty on the ground that (1) the term was not clearly

---

[79] *Printpak v AGF* [1999] Lloyd's Rep IR 542.

[80] *Houghton v Trafalgar Insurance Co Ltd* [1954] 1 QB 247.

[81] Michael Parkington, Nicholas Legh Jones, *MacGillivray & Parkington on Insurance Law* (8th edn, Sweet & Maxwell 1988).

[82] [2000] Lloyd's Rep IR 47; See also Baris Soyer, *Warranties in Marine Insurance* (2nd edn, Cavendish, 2006).

[83] [2000] Lloyd's Rep IR 47, 48.

enough to be stipulated as a continuing warranty, due to the fact that the words "it is warranted that" had multiple linguistic interpretations; and (2) suspensive condition aiming at reducing policy risks could be seen as more suitable for this case.[84]

3.3 The reform of warranty in the Act

There are three major reforms of the concept of warranty in the Act. First, the "basis of contract" clause is repealed. The abolition of the basis of the contract clauses is common and generally supported.[85] The assured's answers in an application form or other information offered by the assured and his broker should be merely considered as representations under the duty of fair presentation rather than warranties.

Second, a warranty can be regarded as "a suspensive condition" or one kind of the condition precedent which "does not relate to a specific claim but is of general application"[86] now, since the obligation of the insurer under the policy is only suspended during the period when the assured does not comply with the warranty. The consequence is that the automatic discharge of the insurer's liability will no longer exist when a warranty is breached. There is no logical reason why the breach of warranty cannot be remedied and the effect of the breach should last forever.[87] The Act encourages the assured to take the initiative to fix problems as soon as possible. Such reform is also in line with the need of legal prac-

---

[84]Ibid, 49, 50.

[85]Parliament, 'Annex A: Support for reform' <http://www.parliament.uk/documents/impact-assessments/IA14-19B.pdf >, accessed 6 May 2015.

[86]Airmic, 'Conditions precedent in insurance Policies' (Airmic technical 2014) < http://www.airmic.com/system/files/conditions%20precedent_WEB.pdf > accessed 4 May 2015.

[87]Howard Bennett, 'Reflections on values: The Law Commissions' proposals with respect to breach of promissory warranty and pre-formation non-disclosure and misrepresentation in commercial insurance' In Bariş Soyer (editor), *Reforming marine and commercial insurance law* (Informa, 2008).

tice. For example, in *The Lydia Flag*,[88] the words "[i]f these warranties are not complied with, the insurance will be suspended until the warranties are complied with" were inserted into the policy. In addition, the courts are also willing to interpret the wording of the policy described "it is warranted that" as a suspensive condition rather than literal interpretation.[89] There is another benefit: protection offered by the Act can be more practical than provisions in the insurance contract. A "held covered" clause is often included in marine policies by mutual consent to limit an underwriter's right to discharge his responsibility under the policy for breach of warranties under conditions that the policyholder would (a) immediately inform the insurer of the existence of breach when the assured knows of the breach; (b) promise to afford extra premiums against increased risks.[90] The obligation of immediate notice does not provide a reasonable time to the assured but requires the assured to act promptly without any delay,[91] even when the assured does not consider the fact as a breach of warranty.[92] In addition, in *Liberian Insurance Agency Inc. v Mosse* case, Justice Donaldson had the opinion that

> the [assured] could not rely on the "held covered" clause because (a) the clause applied only if the premium to be arranged would be such as could properly be described as a reasonable commercial rate...and (b) neither the third party nor the [assured] ever put

---

[88]*Martin Maritime Ltd. v Provident Capital Indemnity Fund Ltd.* [1998] 2 Lloyd's Rep. 652, 652.

[89]*Kler Knitwear Ltd v Lombard General Insurance Company Ltd* [2000] Lloyd's Rep IR 47; also see Baris Soyer, *Warranties in Marine Insurance* (2nd edn, Cavendish, 2006).

[90]Stanley B. Long, Seattle, Washington, '"Held Covered" Clauses in Marine Insurance Policies' (1957) 24 Ins. Counsel J. 401.

[91]Baris Soyer, *Warranties in Marine Insurance* (2nd ed., Cavendish, 2006).

[92]*Pt Buana Samudra Pratama v Marine Mutual Insurance Association (NZ) Ltd* [2011] 2 Lloyd's Rep. 655.

> the full facts before the [insurer] and sought the protection of the clause.[93]

Under the Act, the result of breach of warranty is not as harsh as before, as a "held covered" clause mainly applies to the duty of fair presentation and acts as a distinct variation of the policy providing an extra protection.[94]

3.4 New need-to-know related to the warranty

Some new concepts in the Act related to warranty should be explained. Section 10(6) of the Act states that

> a case falls within this subsection – (a) if the warranty in question requires that by an ascertainable time something is to be done (or not done), or a condition is to be fulfilled, or something is (or not) to be the case, and (b) that requirement is not complied with.[95]

One is time-specific warranty, which means that there is a deadline for remedying breach of some warranties.

Section 10(2) of the Act states that

> an insurer has no liability under a contract of insurance in respect of any loss occurring, or attributable to something happening, after a warranty (express or implied) in the contract has been breached but before the breach has been remedied.[96]

Section 10(4) of the Act holds that

> subsection (2) does not affect the liability of the insurer in respect of losses occurring, or attributable to

[93][1977] 2 Lloyd's Rep. 560, 568.

[94]*The Star Sea* [1997] 1 Lloyd's Rep 360; and *The Mercandian Continent* [2001] 2 Lloyd's Rep 563.

[95]ss 10(6) Insurance Act 2015.

[96]ss 10(2) Insurance Act 2015.

> something happening – (a) before the breach of warranty, or (b) if the breach can be remedied, after it has been remedied[97]

The second is "attributable to something happening", which

> is intended to cater for the situation in which loss arises as a result of an event which occurred during the period of suspension, but is not actually suffered until after the breach has been 'remedied'.[98]

However, when a warranty which related only to the fact in the past is breached, it cannot be remedied.[99]

3.5 New uncertainties related to the warranty

It is worth noticing that some uncertainties nevertheless remain. First, even though the obligation of the insurer resumes when a breach of warranty is remedied, in special circumstances such a breach could hardly be remedied. Especially in marine insurance, it is difficult to prove the time of breach and remedy.[100]

The second uncertainty is that the Act never touches implied conditions; this may lead to some conflicts. In *Molinos Nacionales v Pohjola Insurance Company Ltd*[101] the Tallinn port was stated in the policy as the place of departure, however the vessel actually departed from another port, named Muuga, which was 3 miles away from Tallinn and shared the same port authority. The judge ruled that the departure from the different port did not seem to

---

[97]ss 10(4) Insurance Act 2015.

[98]Explanatory Notes to the Insurance Bill 2015. Para 90.

[99]Law Commission, 'Insurance Contract Law: Business Disclosure; Warranties, Insurer's Remedies for Fraudulent Claims; and Late Payment'

[100]Ozlem Gurese, 'Reform of construction of insurance contract terms' (2013) 1 JBL 39.

[101]Law Commission, Issues Paper 2, 'Insurance Contract Law: Warranties' (2006) <http://lawcommission.justice.gov.uk/docs/ICL2_Warranties.pdf> accessed 8 May 2015> accessed 8 May 2015

make any difference with the risk. According to Section 11(3) of the Act, the assured should be protected, because the obligation of the insurer does not cease. However, the vessel's alteration of port of departure indeed violates Section 43 of the 1906 Act,[102] which allows the insurer not to bear the risk. This is a situation where some applications of the law are competing, and this question has no answer right now.

Third, the new causation test stated in Section 11 creates some uncertainties, even though it is fully supported by Lord Justice Longmore.[103] Historically, a causation test is not suitable for breach of warranty, as there is no causal requirement between the loss and a relevant warranty.[104] The purpose of Section 11 focuses on reducing a specific set of risks so that breaches of warranty only influence legal responsibilities within the same scope of losses. Indeed, it is unfair if the insurer has a right to refuse to undertake the liability only due to non-compliance with the warranties unrelated to the loss. However, there is doubt whether Section 11 may apply to the whole risk, or whether it is limited to a particular type of risk.[105] For example, when an oil refinery takes out fire insurance, it is hard to define the fire risk as a type of risk or a risk as a whole, so it may lead to the uncertainty of applicability of Section 11. This is unanswerable until new court decisions.

The second uncertainty also relates to the causation test. It is difficult to decide whether non-compliance could increase "the risk

---

[102]S 43 Marine Insurance Act 1906: "[w]here the place of departure is specified by the policy, and the ship instead of sailing from that place sails from any other place, the risk does not attach".

[103]Oral Evidence taken before the special public bill committee on Insurance bill (24 December 2014), Q 25, < http://www.publications.parliament.uk/pa/ld201415/ldselect/ldinsur/81/81.pdf > HL Paper 81, accessed 9 May 2015.

[104]Howard Bennett, 'Reflections on values: The Law Commissions' proposals with respect to breach of promissory warranty and pre-formation non-disclosure and misrepresentation in commercial insurance' In Bariş Soyer (editor), *Reforming marine and commercial insurance law* (Informa, 2008).

[105]Timothy Edmonds, Insurance Bill, House of Commons Library Research Paper, 15/03 20 January 2015.

of loss which actually occurred in the circumstances in which it occurred". The LMA and IUA illustrate an inherent vice of the test in a hypothetical situation.[106] A five-level mortise lock on all doors is warranted by the assured, but there is in fact only a three-level mortise lock installed. If a burglar bursts the door open, the warranty could apply to exclude the insurer's liability; if a burglar breaks in through a window and the test is to be strictly and literally executed, the consequence is that the insurer could not discharge its liability. This test seems odd and the extent to which the test should be enforced is not certain right now.

In conclusion, the reform of the warranty is successful because it has changed the situations in which warranty has been abused, makes the participants easily understand the specific content of a warranty, and encourages the assured to remedy the breach of warranty instead of concealing facts. Although the new causation test may lead to some new uncertainties, the default contents will be supplemented by new precedents.

4. The Third Reform: Fraudulent Claims

According to the fraud statistics announced by the Association of British Insurers, fraudulent claims cause great loss: nearly 1.3 billion pounds in the insurance market in 2013.[107] However, fraudulent claims are not mentioned in the 1906 Act, and this defect has been amended by sections 12 and 13 of the Act. Before the Act, the doubt persisting on the fraudulent claim is that the theoretical basis of the remedy of fraudulent claims is not clear, and in particular whether the remedy provides the insurer with an

[106]Written Evidence taken before the special public bill committee on Insurance bill (24 December 2014), 'Written submissions of the LMA and IUA', < http://www.publications.parliament.uk/pa/ld201415/ldselect/ldinsur/81/81.pdf > HL Paper 81, accessed 9 May 2015

[107]Oral Evidence taken before the special public bill committee on Insurance bill (24 December 2014), < http://www.publications.parliament.uk/pa/ld201415/ldselect/ldinsur/81/81.pdf > HL Paper 81, accessed 9 May 2015

entitlement to avoiding the insurance contract.[108] In the view of the law commission,

> The duty not to make a fraudulent claim has variously been characterised as an implied term of the contract, as a breach of section 17, and as a stand-alone common law rule, based on public policy. The House of Lords has severely criticised the idea that an insurer may avoid the contract from the start, without definitely deciding that the clear words of section 17 do not apply.[109]

As a result, before the Act was enacted, it was uncertain which law and regulation should be dispensed. In *Orakpo v Barclays Insurance Services Co Ltd*,[110] no express term was inserted into the policy; however the judge asserted that the insurance contracts usually implied a fraud term, and in the default areas this term should be implied into the policy due to the support of the previous leading cases. In *The Mercandian Continent*,[111] Lord Justice Longmore looked for the principle of good faith and held that the fraud was so immaterial that the policy should not be avoided. However, in *The Aegeon (No 1)*,[112] Lord Justice Mance (as he then was) held that the common law rule should apply to

---

[108]Malcolm A. Clarke, *Law of Insurance Contracts* (5th edn, Informa, 2006).

[109]Law Commission, Issues Paper 7, 'Insurance Contract Law: The insured's Post-Contract Duty of Good Faith.' <http://www.lawcom.gov.uk/wp-content/uploads/2015/06/ICL7_Insureds_Duty_of_Good_Faith.pdf> accessed 9 May 2015, page vii. Also see *The Star Sea* [2001] UKHL 1 [2003] 1 AC 469.

[110][1994] CLC 373. It worth noticing that this case is no longer good law under *The Star Sea* [2003] 1 AC 469.

[111]*K/S Merc-Scandia xxxxii v Certain Lloyd's Underwriters* [2001] 2 Lloyd's Rep. 563.

[112]*Agapitos v Agnew* [2003] QB 556.

fraudulent claims rather than Section 17 of the 1906 Act.[113] The Act adopts the common law rule as a guide to fraudulent claims.[114] The insurer has no responsibility for the fraud claim after the time of the fraudulent act, and the paid insurance compensation could be reclaimed after the discovery of the fraud.[115] This logic is followed by Lord Hobhouse in *The Star Sea*;[116] namely that the law forbids the malicious claimant to benefit from a fraudulent claim. In *Galloway v Guardian Royal Exchange (UK) ltd*[117] the assured fraudulently exaggerated a claim which was found by the court; the court dismissed the claim, but nevertheless held that such act did not taint any claims before the fraudulent act. This view was also supported by *Fargnoli v GA Bonus Plc*[118] in Scotland. A further remedy provided by the Act, is that the insurer is able to terminate the contract from the time of the conduct of the fraudulent act on the base of the notice of termination.[119]

However, there are also some issues which ought to be added in the Act: the first one being what the consequence will be when a fraudulent claim against the insurer and the assured is made by a third party. Second, the concepts of "fraud", "fraudulent claim" or "fraudulent act" are not defined in the Act; the common insurance participants may be baffled by the scope of these concepts, which are hidden in the common law. Thirdly, fraudulent means and devices as a lesser fraud are not mentioned in the Act, but are left for the courts to decide. Before the Special Public Bill Committee, Lord Justice Longmore gave an example as an explanation of a fraudulent device: where the assured lied to get a more favourable judgment during his trial, this was not a fraudulent claim but a fraudulent device. It may be controversial but better to

---

[113]S 17 Marine Insurance Act 1906: "A contract of marine insurance is a contract based upon the utmost good faith, and, if the utmost good faith be not observed by either party, the contract may be avoided by the other party."

[114]Explanatory Notes to the Insurance Bill 2015, Para 101.

[115]S 12 Insurance Act 2015.

[116][2003] 1 AC 469.

[117][1999] Lloyd's Rep IR 209.

[118][1997] SCLR 12.

[119]S 12(1)(c) Insurance Act 2015.

leave this issue to the court to judge and decide which kinds of penalties should be taken to reduce the interests of the liar.[120]

Section 13 of the Act expands group insurance in detail in order to prevent the situation that an innocent assured may be affected by the other joint assureds' misconducts. This reform foundationally and radically solves the problem that arose in *Direct Line Insurance Plc v Khan*,[121] where the court rejected a recovery from the assured due to the other joint policyholder's fraudulent behaviour. It is unfair for the innocent one to suffer lack of insurance protection, because of the mistakes of others.

In conclusion, it is happy for the Act involving the default regime for fraudulent claims to put a sanction on the fraudster and protect the non-fraudulent parties in a group insurance scheme.

5. Late payment of insurance money

Until the Enterprise Act 2016 came into force, there are no provisions among UK statute law which offer a clear remedy solution to the situation when the insured suffers loss as a result of the insurer's failure to pay valid claims without unreasonable delay. This means that even if payment of an insurance claim is delayed for years, the insured is not able to claim compensation for any additional losses caused by that delay. In Scotland, the courts have accepted that "*there is an implied term that the insurer should assess a claim reasonably quickly and with diligence*".[122] This damage will now be clearly available in the whole of the UK

[120]Oral Evidence taken before the special public bill committee on Insurance bill (24 December 2014), Q 27, < http://www.publications.parliament.uk/pa/ld201415/ldselect/ldinsur/81/81.pdf > HL Paper 81, accessed 9 May 2015

[121][2002] Lloyd's Rep IR 364.

[122]C 259 and 260 Explanatory Notes to the Enterprise Act.

according to Part 5 of the Enterprise Act 2016 on 4 May 2017,[123] where late payment of the claim provision is inserted into the Act.

There are some reasons to support this change. It worth noting that the utmost goal for insurance is to prevent or mitigate the losses of the objects insured in the first place.[124] This goal could not be achieved if the problem of late payment is insolvable. What's more, the principle of good faith should apply to the insurer at this issue on the ground of proposed post contract duties.[125] Unobtainable compensation in late payment has been criticized by scholars for a long time[126] and in many cases. In *Sprung v Royal Insurance (UK) Ltd*,[127] the assured could not gain recovery from the insurer for failure of payment, even if the insurer deliberately withheld the payment which the insurer learned to be due

[123]Ss44 (3) The Enterprise Act, The Enterprise Bill 2015 received Royal Assent on 4 May 2016. The provisions relevant to late payment are those at sections 28 -30, which come into force from 4 May 2017 according to section 44(3).

[124]*Apostolos Konstantine Ventouris v Trevor Rex Mountain (the Italia Express (No 3))* [1992] 2 Lloyd's Rep 281.

[125]Peter Macdonald Eggers, Simon Picken, Patrick Foss, *Good Faith and Insurance Contracts,* (informa, 2010). Although the authors consider that further damages are unavailable according to the current law.

[126]John Birds, *Birds' Modern Insurance Law* (Sweet & Maxwell, 2013); J.R. Birds, 'Case Comment: No damages remedy when insurers unjustifiably repudiate liability' (1997) JBL 368; Peter MacDonald Egger, 'late payment of insurance claims' (2013) LMCLQ 341; Mahfuz, 'A Research to Develop English Insurance Law to Accommodate Islamic Principles' (DPhil thesis, the University of Manchester 2013) <https://www.escholar.manchester.ac.uk/api/datastream?publicationPid=uk-ac-man-scw:206987&datastreamId=FULL-TEXT.PDF> accessed 8 May 2015; Colin Ying, 'Damages for late payment of insurance claim' (2006) LQR 205; Malcolm Clarke, 'compensation for failure to pay money due: a 'blot on English common law jurisprudence' partly removed' (2008) JBL 291; Janan Al-Asady, 'Damages, late payment and indemnity insurance' (2006) JBL 396; Sir Andrew Longmore, 'An insurance contracts act for a new century' (2001) LMCLQ 356.

[127][1999]1 Lloyd's Rep IR 111.

under a policy. Lord Justice Beldam proposed that Parliament should legislate to provide the court with a right to compensate the assured for losses caused by late payment.[128] In *Mandrake Holdings Ltd v Countrywide Assured Group Plc*,[129] Lord Justice Rix recommended that the House of Lords should reconsider the late payment issue.[130]

Part 5 of the Enterprise Act 2016 inserts an implied term into every insurance contract that insurers must pay any sums due regarding the claim within a reasonable time. However, the influence of these provisions needs to be considered. The objective of Part 5 of the Enterprise Act 2016 is to assist and keep the UK insurance industry strong, growing and competitive in the long run. Nonetheless, some have expressed different opinions. Lord Flight, who was supported by the Earl of Kinnoull, argued that the amendment will inevitably increase an extra part of many disputed claims and extra claims costs, and this negative impact may drive capital out of the London insurance market and redirect it into other insurance markets.[131] However, Section 29 of the Enterprise Act 2016 allows commercial negotiation between the insurer and his customer or brokers to contract out the liability for consequential losses, so this negative impact may not be as serious as thought. Not only that; the fundamental purpose of the Enterprise Act 2016 is to support small and medium business, as this group is especially vulnerable to late payment and lacks the market power to request the insurer to pay sums. The positive impact of the amendment seems to outweigh the negatives as a whole.

In addition, there are two major areas of concern that deserve discussion. The first concern is the measurement standard of reasonable time within which the insurer must pay sums. Section 13A (3) of the Act states that

[128]Ibid.

[129][2005] EWCA Civ 840.

[130]Ibid.

[131]Reports on Council Meetings, HC Deb 2 February 2016 c879, < http://www.publications.parliament.uk/pa/ld201516/ldhansrd/text/151102-gc0002.htm>, accessed 19 Oct 2016.

> what is reasonable will depend on all the relevant circumstances, but the following are examples of things which may need to be taken into account-(a)The type of insurance; (b) the size and complexity of the claim; (c) compliance with any relevant statutory or regulatory rules or guidance; (d) factors outside the insurer's control.

This indicates that a court, under the influence of a non-exhaustive list of relevant factors, will have to decide how long is a reasonable time for the insurer to pay sums of the claim. According to the Explanatory Note of the Enterprise Act 2016, a reasonable time will largely depend on investigation and assessment of the claim.[132] All of these signify that the larger and more complicated a claim is, the longer a reasonable time lasts. The Explanatory Note of the Enterprise Act 2016 expresses that "whether the insurer had reasonable grounds is intended to be judged objectively".[133] However, the measurement standard of reasonable time is not clear right now due to the fact that what is reasonable will be determined on a case by case basis because of multi-variable factors. The consequential influence of this is that it is hard for the insurer to redesign his internal standard business process as required to meet compliance with the Act.

The second concern is how to measure compensatory damages of the late payment of the claim. The object of Section 13A of the Act is to give the insured pecuniary compensation for the damage or loss he has suffered, but one important limitation on recovery is the test for remoteness of damage. The formulation of the remoteness of damage in contract is interpreted that at the time of making the contract

> the party who has suffered damage does not have to show that the contract-breaker ought to have contemplated, as being not unlikely, the precise detail of the damage or the precise manner of its happening. It is

[132]Explanatory Note of the Enterprise Act 2016

[133]Ibid, Para. 269.

> enough if he should have contemplated that damage of that kind is not unlikely.[134]

This explains reasonable and foreseeable loss. In *Hadley v Baxendale*[135] the court had the opinion that a non-breaching party was entitled to damages which arose naturally from the breach itself or that were in the reasonable contemplation of the parties at the time of contracting. However, it may be difficult for the assured to prove that at the time of establishment of the insurance contract the insurer has realised that a delay in payment might be "not unlikely" to result in loss and damage. This contemplation of the insurer might depend on commercial sense and contractual terms at the court's discretion.[136]

But further concerns need to be considered. In *John Grimes Partnership Ltd v Gubbins*,[137] a developer of land engaged a consulting engineer to design a development scheme, which was completed with 15 months' delay resulting in a reduction in market value of the property in question. The court supported the developer's claim and allowed him to recover the loss of the reduced value of the property for the reasons that:

1. this type of loss is not too remote if the engineer at time of contract ought to have realised that the value of the property may go up as well as down;[138]
2. a very lengthy delay rather than a few days' delay would cause the loss could not be regarded as an unusual situation.[139]

---

[134]*Christopher Hill Ltd v Ashington Piggeries Ltd* [1969] 3 All E.R. 1496, 1524; *Brown v K.M.R. Services Ltd* [1995] 4 All E.R. 598, 621; *Kpohraror v Woolwich Building Society* [1996] 4 All E.R. 119, 126; *Hadley v Baxendale* (1854) 9 Ex. 341.

[135](1954) 9 Exch 341.

[136]*The Achilleas* [2008] 2 Lloy's Rep. 275.

[137][2013] EWCA Civ 37.

[138]Ibid, para 17.

[139]Ibid, para 29.

Suppose that the insurer, following his internal standard business process, takes a long time, more than 18 months, to determine the validity or quantum of a claim in a major but not complex case or in small but complex case. The insurer objectively pays sums of compensation in delay, but subjectively the insurer does not deliberately or recklessly breach this implied term inserted by the Enterprise Act 2016. In this circumstance, it is still uncertain whether the damage of the loss resulting from a delay in payment may be recovered or not.

In conclusion, the Enterprise Act 2016 provides the assured with a way to seek for a remedy of the late payment issue, although this brand-new provisions may cause some practical difficulties at the very beginning.

6. Conclusion

The Act almost completed two demands for a codification. The first was to restate some of the already existing principles of insurance law and clarify fields that were in doubt; the second was to create entirely new principles. The aspirations of the insurance industry and the theoretical circle are basically satisfied by the Act, although some uncertainties still remain to be cleared up in the future. The Act has provided the assured with opportunities to achieve an equal bargaining position with the insurer and to balance the duties between the insurer and the assured. It could be reasonably believed that the Act supplemented by the Enterprise Act 2016 is expected to be in a leading position among the world. Overall, the reform is a triumph and provides hope of maintaining the leading status of English insurance law among the world, although uncertainties as regards some technical points still exist.

Works Cited

Primary Sources

Legislation

Insurance Act 2015
Marine Insurance Act 1906
Enterprise Act 2016
Statutory instruments
Explanatory Notes to the Insurance Bill 2015
Explanatory Notes to the Enterprise Act 2016

Case Law

Achilleas, The. See Transfield Shipping Inc v Mercator Shipping Inc [2008] 2 Lloyd's Rep.275.

Agapitos v Agnew [2003] QB 556.

Banque Keyser v Skandia [1990] 2 Lloyd's Rep 377.

Brown v K.M.R. Services Ltd [1995] 4 All E.R. 598.

Carter v Boehm (1766) 3 Burr 1905, 1 Wm Bl 593.

Christopher Hill Ltd v Ashington Piggeries Ltd [1969] 3 All E.R. 1496.

C.T.I. Inc v Oceanus [1984] 1 Lloyd's Rep 476.

De Hahn v Hartley (1786) I Term Rep 343.

Direct Line Insurance Plc v Khan [2002] Lloyd's Rep IR 364.

Drake Insurance plc v Provident Insurance plc [2003] EWCA Civ 1834.

Galloway v Guardian Royal Exchange (UK) ltd [1999] Lloyd's Rep IR 209.

Genesis Housing Association Ltd v Liberty Syndicate Management Ltd [2013] EWCA Civ 1173.

Provincial Insurance Co. v. Morgan [1933] A.C. 240.

Hadley v Baxendale (1854) 9 Exch 341.

Hewitt Brothers v Wilson. [1915] 2 K.B. 739.

Houghton v Trafalgar Insurance Co Ltd [1954] 1 QB 247.

Hussain v brown [2001] 2 Lloyd's Rep 161.

Ionides v Pacific Fire & Mar Ins Co (1891) L. R. 6 Q. B. 674.

Iron Trades Mutual insurance Co v Companhia de Seguros Imperio [1992] 1 Re. L. R. 213.

Italia Express (No.3), The. See Apostolos Konstantine Ventouris v Trevor Rex Mountain [1992] 2 Lloyd's Rep 281.

John Grimes Partnership Ltd v Gubbins [2013] EWCA Civ 37.

K/S Merc-Scandia xxxxii v Certain Lloyd's Underwriters [2001] 2 Lloyd's Rep. 563.

Kler Knitwear Ltd v Lombard General Insurance Company Ltd [2000] Lloyd's Rep IR 47, 48.

Kpohraror v Woolwich Building Society [1996] 4 All E.R. 119.

Lambert v Cooperative Insurance Society Ltd [1957] 2 Lloyd's Rep 485.

Liberian Insurance Agency Inc. v Mosse [1977] 2 Lloyd's Rep. 560.

Litsion Pride, The. See Black King Shipping Corporation v Massie [1985] 1 Lloyd's Rep 437.

Mar Rich & Co v Portman [1997] 1 Lloyd's Rep 225.

Martin Maritime Ltd. v Provident Capital Indemnity Fund Ltd. [1998] 2 Lloyd's Rep. 652, 652.

Mandrake Holdings Ltd v Countrywide Assured Group Plc [2005] EWCA Civ 840.

Mercandian Continent, The. See K/S Merc-Scandia xxxxii v Certain Lloyd's Underwriters and Ocean Marine Insurance Co. Ltd. and Others [2001] 2 Lloyd's Rep 563.

Orakpo v Barclays Insurance Services Co Ltd [1994] CLC 373.

Overseas Commodities Ltd v Style [1958] 1 Lloyd's Rep. 546.

Pan Atlantic Insurance Co Ltd v Pine Top Insurance Co Ltd [1995] 1 AC 501.

Printpak v AGF [1999] Lloyd's Rep IR 542.

Proudfoot v Montefiore (1867) LR 2 QB 511.

Pt Buana Samudra Pratama v Marine Mutual Insurance Association (NZ) Ltd [2011] 2 Lloyd's Rep. 655.

Seaman v Fonereau (1743) 2 Stra 1183.

Sprung v Royal Insurance (UK) Ltd [1999]1 Lloyd's Rep IR 111.

St Paul Fire and Marine Insurance Co Ltd v McConnell Dowell Constructors Ltd [1995] 2 Lloyd's Rep 116.

Thomson v Weems (1884) 9 App. Cas. 671.

The Fargnoli v GA Bonus Plc [1997] SCLR 12.

The Star Sea [2003] 1 AC 469.

The Star Sea [1997] 1 Lloyd's Rep 360.
Tonkin v UK insurance Ltd [2006] 2 ALL ER (Comm) 550.
Whiten v Pilot Insurance Co [2002] 1 SCR 595.
Wise Ltd. v. Grupo Nacional Provincial S.A. [2004] 2 Lloyd's Rep. 483.
Zurich General Accident and Liability Insurance Co v Leven 1940 SC 406.

Official materials

House of Commons, Briefing Paper of Enterprise Bill [HL] 2015-16, (No. CBP 7485, 2016).
Law Commission, Insurance Law Non-Disclosure and Breach of Warranty (Law Com No 104, 1980).
Law Commission, Insurance Contract Law: Misrepresentation, Non-Disclosure and Breach of Warranty by the inusred (Law Com CP No 182 2007).
Law commission, Insurance Contract Law: The Business Insured's Duty of Disclosure and the Law of Warranties (Law Com CP No 204, 2012).
Law Commission, Consumer Insurance Law: pre-contract disclosure and misrepresentation (Law Com No 319, 2009).
Law Commission, Insurance Contract Law: Business Disclosure; Warranties, Insurers's Remedies for Fraudulent Claims; and Late Payment (Law Com No 353 2014).
Law Commission, Issues Paper 1, Insurance Contract Law: Misrepresentation and Non-Disclosure (2006).
Law Commission, Issues Paper 2, Insurance Contract Law: Warranties (2006).
Law Commission, Issues Paper 3, Intermediaries and Pre-contract Information (2007).
Law Commission, Issues Paper 6, Insurance Contract Law: Damages for late Payment and the Insurer's Duty of Good Faith (2010).
Law Commission, Issues Paper 7, Insurance Contract Law: The insured's Post-Contract Duty of Good Faith (2010).
Mactavish, 'Special public bill Committee on the insurance bill – evidence' (2014).

Oral Evidence taken before the special public bill committee on Insurance bill (2014).

Timothy Edmonds, Insurance Bill, House of Commons Library Research Paper (2015).

The Lloyd's Market Association and The International Underwriting Association of London, 'Written submissions of the LMA and IUA' (2014).

Written Evidence taken before the special public bill committee on Insurance bill (2014), 'Memorandum submitted by Lord Newby, Minster in charge of the bill', HL Paper 81.

Secondary Sources

Books

B. John, L. Ben, M. Simon, *MacGillivray on Insurance Law* (12th ed., Sweet & Maxwell, 2012).

B. John, *Birds' Modern Insurance Law* (Sweet & Maxwell, 2013).

G. Jonathan, M. Robert, B. Claire, T. Mark, *Arnould's law of marine insurance and average* (18th ed, Sweet & Maxwell, 2013).

H.Susan, *Law of Marine Insurance* (Routledge-Cavendish, 1996).

M. E. Peter, P. Simon, F. Patrick, *Good Faith and Insurance Contracts*, (Informa, 2010).

P. Michael, L. J.Nicholas, *MacGillivray & Parkington on Insurance Law* (8th ed. Sweet & Maxwell 1988).

S. Baris, *Warranties in Marine Insurance* (2nd ed, Cavendish, 2006).

Articles and Essays

A. Janan, 'Damages, late payment and indemnity insurance' (2006) *JBL* 396.

B. Howard, 'Reflections on values: The Law Commissions' proposals with respect to breach of promissory warranty and pre-formation non-disclosure and misrepresentation in commercial insurance' In Bariş Soyer (ed.), *Reforming marine and commercial insurance law (Informa, 2008).*

B. L. Stanley , Seattle, Washington, '"Held Covered" Clauses in Marine Insurance Policies' (1957) 24 *Ins. Counsel J.* 401.

C. Malcolm, 'compensation for failure to pay money due: a 'blot on English common law jurisprudence' partly removed' (2008) *JBL* 291.

H. John, 'The Omnipotent Warranty: England v The World' in Marc Huybrechts and others (eds), *Marine Insurance at the Turn of the Millennium* (Intersentia, 1999).

J.R. Birds, 'Case Comment: No damages remedy when insurers unjustifiably repudiate liability' (1997) *JBL* 368.

L. Andrew, 'An insurance contracts act for a new century' (2001) *LMCLQ* 356.

M. E. Peter, 'late payment of insurance claims' (2013) *LMCLQ* 341.

M. Robert, C. Colin, 'Doubts about insurance codes' (2001) *JBL* 587.

R. A. Hasson, 'the "basis of the Contract Clause" in insurance law' (1971) 34(1) *MLR* 29.

Y. Colin, 'Damages for late payment of insurance claim' (2006) *LQR* 205.

International Resources

Airmic, 'Conditions precedent in insurance Policies' (Airmic technical 2014) < http://www.airmic.com/system/files/conditions%20precedent_WEB.pdf> accessed 4 May 2015.

Carl Christian Rösiö, 'Warranties in marine insurance: an unpleasant necessity?' (Juridisk Publikation, 2010) <http://juridiskpublikation.se/wp-content/uploads/2014/10/12010_Carl-Christian-R%C3%B6si%C3%B6.pdf> 4 May 2015.

Mahfuz, 'A Research to Develop English Insurance Law to Accommodate Islamic Principles' (DPhil thesis, the University of Manchester 2013) <https://www.escholar.manchester.ac.uk/api/datastream?publicationPid=uk-ac-man-scw:206987&datastreamId=FULL-TEXT.PDF> accessed 8 May 2015

Mactavish, 'Corporate risk & insurance the case for placement reform' (the Mactavish Protocals, 2011) <http://www.airmic.-com/system/files/Corporate%20Risk%20-

%20Placement%20Reform%20EXECUTIVE%20SUMMARY.pdf> accessed 28 May 2015.

M. Rob, 'Reforming Insurance Law: Is there a case for reverse transportation?' < http://lawcommission.justice.gov.uk/docs/ICL_Merkin_report.pdf> 4 May 2015.

Violence Against Women in Palestine and Mediocre Accountability

Tamara Tawfiq Tamimi[1]

Violence Against Women (VAW) is a worldwide pervasive phenomenon. This submission makes use of a variety of primary and secondary resources; such as legislation, international law instruments, official statistics, books and book chapters, and journal articles. The focus on VAW will be in the Palestinian context, with occasional reference to "honour" crimes where appropriate. The article will commence in covering the main points of convergence and divergence in the literature available on VAW and "honour" crimes. Further, the occurrence and prevalence of VAW - in Palestine - will be situated and analysed within the social, economic and legal dimensions of patriarchy. An in-depth, critical analysis of the impact of colonialism and neo-liberalism/ capitalism will be employed to deconstruct the factors that underpin VAW. Moreover, this section will highlight the persistence of VAW; shedding light on the absence of alternatives, for women survivors of violence and the role of the legal system. For the purposes of critically engaging with VAW, exclusive focus will be dedicated to the treatment of the penal code applied in Palestinian courts of HRV, and crimes in the Palestinian society. The final part of the paper will tackle "law" as a medium to ad-

[1]MA Human Rights Law, SOAS, University of London; Executive Editor of SOAS Law Journal (Volume 3, Issue 1).

dress VAW, highlighting its importance through showcasing the impact of legal reform efforts—a temporal analysis of progress within this parameter will be employed. To further vindicate the need for comprehensive action in pursuance of gender equality, complementary strategies that feed into the "prevent" component of the due diligence standard, as well as the transformative equality concept of the gender mainstreaming model will be presented; including educational reform, economic empowerment, and rehabilitation of perpetrators. Thus, seeking to identify possible answers for the reasons that make legal reform insufficient to eliminate VAW, and thereafter determine necessary strategies to complement legal reform.

Keywords: Violence Against Women, Palestine, Equality, Civil Society.

1. Introduction

Violence against women (VAW) is a worldwide phenomenon that is underpinned by different contextual factors. These factors serve to maintain, reinforce or feed into the imbalance in the power relations between men and women. This in turn, complements and extends the disproportionate impact of the masculinity and patriarchy of the global order on women.

Although violence is generally associated with its physical dimension, it nevertheless takes many different forms. Despite the absence of an international convention on VAW, General Recommendation (GR) 19 of the Committee on the Elimination of all forms of Discrimination Against Women, elaborates VAW as a subset of discrimination including deprivation of enjoyment of human rights and fundamental freedoms, and inequality in distribution of and access to resources.[2] Additionally, the United Nations General Assembly Declaration on the Elimination of Violence Against Women follows a highly similar approach. It stresses that VAW is a major impediment to the realisation of equality, development and peace.[3] A further milestone was the creation and appointment in 1994; of the first Special Rapporteur on Violence Against Women, its Causes and Consequences. Both GR 19 and Declaration define VAW as "violence directed against a woman, because she is a woman or that affects women disproportionately". Despite the narrowness in the scope and generality of the phrasing, this definition offers a useful tool to acclimatise different forms of VAW and interpret them within their wider political, economic, social and legal contexts.

The three aforementioned international advancements in terms of acknowledgements of VAW were followed with regional ones that cumulatively expanded and deepened understanding of VAW. The first regional convention on VAW was the Convention of Bellum do Para (Inter-American Convention), adopted in 1994. The Convention is very similar structurally, to both GR 19 and UNGA Declaration. It has not only identified the scope of violence within the sphere of the physical, sexual and psychological harm incurred in both the public and private sphere, but also determined, in Article 9, intersectional factors that further disadvantage and oppress women. The absence of an African convention specifically on VAW is due to the drafting of the Protocol to the African Charter on Human and Peoples' Rights, on the Rights of Women in Africa (African Protocol herein) in 2003, at a time where VAW was a major issue that received constant attention in the international arena and as such was integrated into the protocol itself. This is worthy of attention as Article 1 of the African Protocol expanded the scope of violence beyond physical, sexual and

---

[2]UN Committee for the Elimination of All Forms of Discrimination against Women, 'General Recommendation No 19' in 'Note by the Secretariat, Compilation of General Comments and General Recommendations Adopted by Human Rights Treaty Bodies' (29 July 1994) UN Doc HRI/GEN/1/Rev.1.

[3]Declaration on the Elimination of Violence Against Women (adopted 20 December 1993 UNGA Resolution 48/104) preamble 1.

psychological to include economic harm. Another interesting aspect of the approach of the African Protocol to VAW is expanding its interpretation to include an infringement on and violation of many recognised rights, such as right to dignity in Article 3, right to life integrity and security in Article 4, and elimination of harmful practices in Article 5. Furthermore, VAW is highlighted in intersectional provisions, such as protection in armed conflict in Article 11, protection of elderly women in Article 22 and protection of women with disability in Article 23. Regional legal instruments were completed with the Council of Europe Convention on Preventing and Combating Violence Against Women and Domestic Violence. The Convention builds on the accumulation of wealth from previous international and regional instruments, moving beyond protection by instating empowerment mechanisms that enable women to counter violence they are subjected to.

Professors Hilary Charlesworth, Christine Chinkin and Shelley Wright describe in their 1991 ground-breaking paper 'Feminist Approaches to International Law' the three-fold intersectional exclusion of women from the global south in decision-making and policy formulation processes. They explain that the first layer comes at the global level of exclusion of global south countries from global politics. The second layer comes at a national level of exclusion of women by their countrymen. The third layer manifests of the marginalization of the voices of global south women by global north women within the global feminist movement.[4] This analysis, despite being acclimatised within a political participation framework, is a useful tool to analyse the disproportionate impact of several intersectional factors in the subjecting and perpetuating VAW in Palestine. The obvious factors in this sense are gender and culture, with less importance attributed to social class, place of residency (rural/urban), and economic status - all of which will be explored in this paper.

Palestinian women were expected to and did play an instrumental role in national liberation and resistance, and to a lesser extent in State building, following the establishment of the Pales-

---

[4]Hilary Charlesworth, Christine Chinkin and Shelley Wright, 'Feminist Approaches to International Law' (1991) 85 American Journal of International Law 613, 619.

tinian Authority (PA). However, in light of a multitude of factors that will be elaborated in the body of this paper, VAW goes unacknowledged in terms of criminalisation and employment of public resources to addressing it; for example, over the past 20 years, the Palestinian Central Bureau of Statistics undertook only one survey on violence in the Palestinian society. On reflection of results, 37% of Palestinian women were subjected to at least one form of violence, including psychological (58.6%), physical (23.5%), sexual (11.8%), social (54.8%), and economic (55.1%).[5]

2. Key Literature

Different contexts and theoretical perspectives give rise to a variety of definitions, forms of and factors informing VAW. For example, the sociological definition highlights the mentality and psyche of the perpetrator, stating "the illegal employment of methods of physical coercion for personal or group ends...which is distinct from force or power;".[6] Alternatively, the socio-psychological definition encompasses both the physical and psychological aspects of violence, stating "a form of human aggression that involves inflicting physical damage on persons or property".[7] The many definitions of VAW are all equally viable as they highlight or showcase the most relevant aspect of discrimination against women to the desired context within a VAW framework. Accordingly, this is one of the strongest aspects of the generic international definition of VAW given in GR 19 and the UNGA Declaration.

---

[5]PCBS, *Violence in the Palestinian Society Survey* (PCBS 2011) >http://www.pcbs.gov.ps/Portals/_Rainbow/Documents/vio_a.htm<.

[6]Preeti Misra, *Domestic Violence Against Women: Legal Control and Judicial Response* (Deep & Deep Publications 2007) 44.

[7]Ibid 46.

Irrespective of the employed definition, VAW is pervasive[8] to the extent that it is considered a universal phenomenon.[9] It usually takes place at the hands of the husband, father, brother, son and father-in-law[10] - and is affected in terms of type and frequency; by a number of different factors, including class, geographic location, and culture[11]. A different set of scholarly work attributes VAW to a whole different set of factors, including inferiority perceptions, poverty, limited education, employment and equality opportunities, and absence of deterrent laws.[12]

VAW takes many different forms and is not only limited to physical violence; it extends to include sexual, psychological and emotional abuse;[13] other resources extend this classification to include economic and social violence. Whereas economic violence refers to the deprivation of women from enjoying and accessing resources - including forbidding her from working, seizing her salary, forcing her to sell valuables and property and depriving her of inheritance - social violence refers to attempts to impose social restrictions on women and girls and limit their chances of communication - it infringes on other forms of internationally recognised rights; including freedom of movement and privacy to name a few.[14] Different resources identify different acts within the aforementioned categories of violence; while some references name murder, wife-beating, female infanticide and foeticide, kidnapping and abduction, custodial and public assault and mutilation torture under physical violence,[15] other resources - depend-

---

[8]Subhash Chandra Singh, 'Gender Violence: Some Contextual Issues' in K Uma Devi (ed.), Violence Against Women: Human Rights Perspective (Serials Publications 2005) 21.

[9]Women's Affairs Technical Committee, Gaps, Challenges and Opportunities in the Services System Provided to Women Survivors of Gender Based Violence in the Gaza Strip Study (Alianza por la Solidaridad 2014), 24.

[10]Singh, (n 7) 22.

[11]Ibid, 21.

[12]Women's Affairs Technical Committee, (n 8) 28.

[13]Singh, (n 7) 21.

[14]Women's Affairs Technical Committee, (n 8) 27

[15]Ibid.

ing on their context - omit some of the aforementioned forms, restricting physical violence to kidnapping and abduction, bride burning, wife-beating and murder.[16]

Similarly, the frameworks utilised to theoretically qualify and explain VAW vary significantly; one resource focuses on the disproportionate disadvantage of the psychological factor, social exclusion, economic dependence of women over men, and the biological factor of child bearing, which instantaneously places women in an inferior position to men.[17] Another set of theorems focus exclusively on qualifying domestic violence; including through the use of the social problem approach, family system theory, psychological theory, physiological theory, psycho-pathological theory, socio-cultural theories, multifactor theory[18] and socio-psychological theory.[19]

"Honour" related violence (HRV) and crimes face the same pluralistic definitions VAW is afforded; however, one crosscutting component in the definition of HRV and crimes is a perception of transcending socially-imposed sexual norms by a woman.[20] Internationally, issues pertaining to HRV and crimes have received less scrutiny compared with other forms of VAW – predominantly, this is due to cultural relativism employment argument, where "cultural" and "traditional" practices require tolerance and respect.

---

[16]Ram Ahuja, *Violence Against Women* (Rawat Publications 2003) 93, 121, 151, 182.

[17]Singh (n 7) 25-27.

[18]Misra (n 5) 227-251.

[19]Ahuja (n 15) 203.

[20]Mohammad Mazher Idriss, 'Honour, Violence, Women and Islam-An Introduction' in Mohammad Mazher Idriss and Tahir Abbas (eds) (Routledge Taylor and Francis Group 2011) 1;
Heidi Safia Mirza and Veena Meetoo, '"There Is Nothing 'Honourable' about Honour Killings": Gender, Violence and the Limits of Multiculturalism' in Mohammad Mazher Idriss and Tahir Abbas (eds), *Honour, Violence, Women and Islam* (Routledge Taylor and Francis Group 2011) 42;
Lynn Welchman and Sarah Hossain, 'Introduction: "Honour", Rights and Wrongs' in Lynn Welchman and Sarah Hossain (eds), *'Honour': Crimes, Paradigms, and Violence against Women* (Zed Books 2005) 5.

One misconception and stereotype about HRV is the restriction of its geographic scope to Middle Eastern and Muslim societies; HRV permeates all religions and social classes, such that several resources elaborate its occurrence in the UK and across Europe, in addition to the production of official reports, by the Special Rapporteur on Violence Against Women, its Causes and Consequences in several Western secular states, such as Brazil, Denmark, Israel, Netherlands, Sweden and Turkey.[21]

These occurrences are directly related to the control of women's sexuality,[22] under the pretext of "preservation of honour"; these regulations and restrictions are a severe infringement on women's human rights, including control of their own lives, freedom of expression, association, movement, and bodily integrity.[23] Nonetheless, several mitigations and reforms are suggested to overcome and address issues pertaining to HRV, including legislative and other legal reforms, preventative and protective reforms.[24]

3. VAW in Palestine: Overview

Oppression of and violence against women is a direct manifestation of patriarchy and masculinity that perceives women as an auxiliary to men; such that Palestinian women are seen as mothers, daughters or wives but not as independent human beings, whose existence is worthy of acknowledgement without an attachment to a male counterpart. A multitude of factors either maintain or perpetuate this patriarchy, including societal oppression, economic dependence and the public/private divide.

Patriarchy and masculinity in Palestinian society take many different manifestations, including the perception that the locus of

[21] Radhika Coomaraswamy, 'Preface: Violence Against Women and "Crimes of Honour"' in Lynn Welchman and Sara Hossain (eds), *'Honour': Crimes, Paradigms, and Violence against Women* (Zed Books 2005) xii.

[22] Welchman and Hossain (n 19) 2.

[23] Coomaraswamy (n 20) xi.

[24] Welchman and Hossain (n 19) 8, 11, 13.

family "honour" is women's bodies, giving rise to immense discretion in interpretation and control of women's sexuality and regulation of women's sexual activity.[25] The second relevant manifestation of societal masculinity, pertains to the responsibility thrust on and shouldered by men - in order to "provide" for and "protect" their families.[26]

3.1 Societal Oppression

Postcolonial theories postulate that dominant groups exercise their dominance and strength over weaker groups in colonial and postcolonial times.[27] The Israeli occupation of the West Bank - since 1967 and its associated system of oppression - has led to the emergence of subsequent forms of resistance. This interlocked system of oppression and resistance has led to the legitimisation of an atmosphere of violence.

In this context, Palestinian men subject Palestinian women and children to different forms of violence.[28] This is further substantiated by the increased levels of VAW since the outbreak of the second Palestinian Intifada (uprising) in 2000.[29] The second Palestinian Intifada came against the backdrop of the hopeful period of 1993-1999, where the peace process between the Palestinian Liberation Organisation and the government of Israel was flourishing and progressing. During this period, Palestinians had high hopes for political stability and subsequent economic prosperity. The beginning of the second Intifada entailed the crashing

---

[25]Coomaraswamy (n 20) xi.

[26]UNCHR 'Report of the Special Rapporteur on Violence Against Women, its Causes and Consequences, Yakin Ertürk: Mission to Occupied Palestinian Territory' (2 February 2005) UN Doc E/CN.4/2005/72/Add.4, 8.

[27]Bell Hooks, *We Real Cool: Black Men and Masculinity* (Routledge: New York and London 2004) 47.

[28]Shadia El Sarraj, 'Screaming in Silence' in Marguerite R. Waller and Jennifer Rycenga (eds), *Frontline Feminisms: Women, War, and Resistance* (Taylor & Francis 2001) 18.

[29]Lynn Welchman, 'Honour and Violence Against Women in a Modern Shar'i Discourse' (2007) 5 HAWWA 2.

down of these dreams, with re-emerging feelings of insecurity and instability; even though Palestinians have experienced these feelings before, they never did with such intensity against the backdrop of hope generated during this period of supposed transition towards statehood. This uncertainty, coupled with other factors of economic and social nature, has led to a severe escalation in internal levels and rates of VAW.

3.2 Economic Dependence

VAW in the Palestinian society in particular was further exacerbated by the deteriorating economic situation in Palestine. Generally, Palestinian women are economically dependent on Palestinian men, and Palestinian men are unable to conform to social expectations and fulfil their responsibilities of providing for their families. The indefinite temporality, in transition from occupation towards statehood, has contributed significantly to the failure of the PA in creating a viable economy and sustainable job opportunities, thus maintaining sky rocketing rates of unemployment, which stand at 23.4% (20.6% for males and 35% for females) in 2013.[30] This is further aggravated when taking a close look at the poverty levels, such that 25.8% and 12.9% of the Palestinians live under the poverty line and in deep poverty, respectively in 2011.[31] It is important to clarify here that high rates of unemployment and poverty were observed before the establishment of the PA, however, these families were supported through a "collective" element in the Palestinian social fabric that served as an alternative complementary system of social security at the time. This "collective" element was informed in a unified recognition of the role of the occupation in maintaining high levels of economic instability, and a consolidated unitary front in resisting this occupation; one by-product of resistance was the lack of focus on finances, such that extended family members and the community of Palestinians who could not afford to secure the basic needs of livelihood provided

[30]Palestinian Central Bureau of Statistics, *Palestine Statistical Yearbook 2014* (PCBS 2014) 127.

[31]Ibid, 115.

both financial support and basic commodities to facilitate their livelihood.

One of the tasks of the PA was to build state institutions and a viable economy; economic policy led to the establishment of a liberal, open-market economic system, necessitating an ability to access natural resources and control exports and imports, which are non-existent in light of the continued occupation. The neoliberal economic system, coupled with an indefinite temporality in transition, have led to the emergence of different needs and priorities among the Palestinian society; effectively compromising the "collective" element of the social fabric, and shifting the characteristic component to an individualistic liberal focus.

A longstanding view on women's employment, in line with the patriarchal perception that women's rightful place is the house to provide and care for male members of the family, is that Palestinian women should seek and be granted employment as a last resort to economic "need"; consequently, women's employment was never perceived as a human right. This perception, coupled with limited work opportunities, has led to a striking employment gap in the Palestinian labour market - with men's participation standing at 69.3%, compared with 17.3% women's participation in 2013.[32] Furthermore, 80.2% of the working women are employed in the agriculture and fishing industry (20.9%) and service delivery branches (59.3%):[33] two of the lowest paying sectors and industries. These different factors make Palestinian women economically dependent on men, thereby rendering men the main power holders in the marital/ familial relationship.[34]

3.3. Private/Public Divide in the Legal System:

Another shortcoming in the performance of the PA was their failure to consolidate a unified Palestinian legal system, in light of the hybrid legal system in place from previous colonial rules; such

---

[32]Ibid, 127.

[33]PCBS, Women and Men in Palestine: Issues and Statistics (PCBS 2014) 58.

[34]Jan Pahl, 'Patterns of Money Management within Marriage' (1980) 9 Journal of Social Policy 313, 315.

that it consists of a combination of Ottoman, British, Jordanian, Egyptian, Israeli (military orders) and Palestinian legislation. Opting for refraining to modernise and unify the Palestinian legal system has been instrumental in the flourish of patriarchy and masculinity, particularly in light of the presence of laws that severely discriminate against women on the de jure and de facto levels.

The family is considered the basic unit of the society, with family affairs, issues and problems considered a private matter instead of a public matter, in line with Islamic *shari'a* and discourse. This private distinction extends to include mediocre state interference in family affairs, which are legally regulated through an Islamic *shari'a*-based Personal Status Law (PSL). One of the many facets of discrimination against women in this law is the regulation of marital affairs. The approach followed in the drafting of the marriage contract, effectively marginalises the importance for women's consent to engage in sexual intercourse with their husbands, and consequently, marital rape frequently occurs and at high rates. The majority of these cases go unreported due to an association with a prevalent social stigma that shames women for unfulfilling their marital duties and responsibilities.[35] Nonetheless, at least 11.8% of Palestinian women have reported in the aforementioned PCBS survey that they have been subjected to sexual violence.[36]

Notwithstanding the problematic aspects of the PSL, this is duplicated by virtue of the criminal codes that apply in the West Bank "Jordanian Penal Code 16 of 1960" and Gaza Strip "British Mandate Penal Code 74 of 1936". These two sets of laws reinforce the injustice that is already in place by the PSL, as they do not criminalise VAW, including domestic violence and marital

[35]Interview with Soraida Abed Hussein, General Director of Women's Affairs Technical Committee (Ramallah, Palestine, 23 December 2015)

[36]PCBS, *Violence in the Palestinian Society Survey* (PCBS 2011) >http://www.pcbs.gov.ps/Portals/_Rainbow/Documents/vio_a.htm<

rape.[37] These laws further reflect and strengthen societal masculinity and patriarchy in providing extenuating circumstances and reduced sentences to perpetrators of "honour" crimes. While Article 340 of the Jordanian Penal Code of 1960 was very rarely used in the Palestinian legal system - due to the difficulty of proving the circumstances that would qualify the perpetrator to an extenuating circumstance - Articles 97 and 99 of the same legal text have been used to obtain reduced sentences; most frequently, Article 98 has been used extensively in obtaining extenuating circumstances, whereas the defence had to prove that the defendant was in a fit of rage as a reaction to an unlawful or dangerous act committed by the victim at the time of committing the murder. A suspicion of the committing of adultery or engaging in extramarital sexual relations is indisputably considered an unlawful or dangerous act in both the Palestinian and Jordanian legal systems.[38] These extenuating circumstances and reduced sentences, and their relative ease of qualification have been used by Palestinian men to "discipline" their wives, sisters and daughters, when simple acts of defiance, considered a challenge of manhood took place - compromising their authority and control.[39] Many other cases in recent years, where these provisions have been "misused", include cases of inheritance; the absence of legal penalties for perpetrators of so-called "honour" crimes have encouraged family members to kill women who demand their rightful inheritance in their father's and mother's estates and property; thereafter, using the aforementioned legal provisions in order to eventually receive a reduced sentence of up to two years, and a sizeable inheritance. In these cases, the absence of

---

[37]Women's Centre for Legal Aid and Counselling, *Right to Life Denied: Killing of Women in Palestine Social Reality and the Law 2011-2012* (Women's Centre for Legal Aid and Counselling 2013) 24.

[38]Ibid, 25-26

[39]Aida Touma-Sliman, 'Culture, National Minority, and the State: Working against the "Crime of Honour" within the Palestinian Community in Israel' in Lynn Welchman and Sara Hossain (eds.), *'Honour': Crimes, Paradigms, and Violence against Women* (Zed Books 2005) 181.

legal accountability connects firstly to an infringement and a compromise of the right to life, and secondly on social and economic rights of Palestinian women.

3.4 Absence of Alternatives

The frequency of acts such as marital rape and "honour" crimes, their limited reporting (in the case of marital rape) and the absence of deterrent laws in the penal code are effectively internalising these practices into Palestinian culture and norms. These practices persist due to the absence of alternatives for Palestinian women, and the subsequent imposition on Palestinian women to contend with their realities. A very small portion of the Palestinian women are economically independent and able to take the decision of leaving their violent husbands and leading their own lives. Those who do so still need to consider the social stigma of returning to their family house, as social norms find it impermissible for the majority of these women to live by themselves, conditioning their divorce with returning to the family home to ensure that the family "honour" remains intact. Another reason for women's silence about the oppression that they face is fear from portraying the Palestinian people as a violent, barbaric society, and extending that portrayal to compromise their legitimate right to statehood and self-determination. This renders the suffering of Palestinian women on two levels; they have to face the patriarchal national "self", and the oppressive foreign "other".

4. The Way Forward

4.1 Legal Reform

Palestinian civil society organisations (CSOs) have been working relentlessly for the past 25 years on addressing VAW. Their efforts can be categorised into service delivery, awareness-raising and advocacy and lobbying. CSOs, complementing official institutions, provide psychological counselling and legal aid services to women survivors of violence, in addition to delivering awareness-raising workshops for them and for their communities. Also, CSOs consolidate efforts with relevant official institutions, including the Ministry of Women's Affairs (MoWA), Ministry of Social Affairs (MoSA) and Ministry of Justice (MoJ); in this context, several official institutions, led by the MoWA collaborated with feminist and human rights organisations in the West Bank and Gaza Strip, as well as United Nations organisations to draft the National Strategy to Combat Violence Against Women 2011-2019.[40] The development of this strategy was further strengthened when the Palestinian Cabinet of Ministers signed 6 Memoranda of Understanding with the Ministry of Health, Ministry of Justice (MoJ), Ministry of Education and Higher Education, Ministry of Interior, Ministry of Social Affairs and the Civil Defence to implement the strategic goals of the strategy.[41]

In addition, mass advocacy campaigns to reform the legal system that allows for VAW have been undertaken. The predominant campaigns focused on the amendment of the PSL and Penal Codes in force in the West Bank and Gaza Strip, through the establishment of coalitions that brought together CSOs and official institutions. The "National Coalition for the Amendment of the Penal Code", comprising CSOs and official institutions, led by the MoJ, drafted an alternative Penal Code to be enacted through a Presidential Decree. This is per Article 43 of the Palestinian Basic Law, which states

> "The President of the National Authority shall have the right, in cases of necessity that cannot be delayed, and when the Legislative Council is not in session, to issue decrees that have the power of law".[42]

In light of the political division between the West Bank and Gaza Strip, and subsequent disruption of the work of the Palestinian

---

[40] 2011-2019 National Strategy to Combat Violence Against Women >http://mowa.pna.ps/English%20Part.pdf< 62-63

[41] General Secretariat of the Council of Ministers Third Quarterly Report >http://www.palestinecabinet.gov.ps/WebSite/Upload/Documents/gov13_q1.pdf< 37

[42] 2003 Amended Basic Law

Legislative Council since June 2007, the Palestinian President Mahmoud Abbas, issued a presidential decree on 15 May 2011, annulling Article 340 of the "Jordanian Penal Code 16 of 1960" and amending Article 18 of the "British Mandate Penal Code 74 of 1936" to exclude "honour" crimes.

Additionally, on 1 April 2014, the PA ratified and acceded to 18 international human rights law and international humanitarian law conventions and treaties, including the Convention on the Elimination of all forms of Discrimination Against Women (CEDAW). When four girls were killed during the period 12 April - 12 May, mass protests organised by civil society and grassroots organisations, complementing the draft Penal Code awaiting adoption, prompted the Palestinian President to issue another presidential decree amending Article 98 of the "Jordanian Penal Code 16 of 1960", to exclude "honour" crimes. Despite these breakthroughs, several articles in this penal code remain discriminatory against Palestinian women, including Articles 97 and 99. To capitalise on the potential of legal reform, advocacy efforts for the adoption of a new penal code that ensures gender equality are imperative.

The ratification of CEDAW and amendment of the penal code were instrumental in protecting Palestinian women - despite their shortcomings. For example, a simple comparison in the data documented by the Women's Centre for Legal Aid and Counselling, of the number of women killed under the pretext of "honour" pre and post ratification of CEDAW, would demonstrate that legal reform and the passage of deterrent laws play a major role in the protection and empowerment of women. For example, the number of cases documented under "honour" crimes reached 102 for the period 2007-2014; with 27 cases documented in each of 2013 and 2014, compared to 16 in 2015. To further substantiate this, once the most used provision in "honour" crimes ruling was amended in 2014, the difference in the number of cases is striking - with 16 cases in the first 4.5 months, at a rate 3.5 cases/ month and 11 in the remaining 7.5 months, at a rate of 1.5 cases/ month.[43] This may be attributed further in light of the absence of international law literacy among the Palestinian people, whereas

[43]Women's Centre for Legal Aid and Counseling Documentation Reports on "Femicide" 2007-2015.

the main conception (or misconception) is that upon the ratification of CEDAW, perpetrators are automatically held legally liable for such crimes.

Efforts on the legal reform front are evidently important to ensure the protection of women and their human rights. Comprehensive programmes of intervention by CSOs, nonetheless, should focus on the sensitisation of all stakeholders to women's rights and the importance of gender parity. One main stakeholder in this sense is *Shari'a* judges, particularly in light of the various interpretations that Islamic laws afford.

The aforementioned cumulative legal breakthroughs undertaken and achieved demonstrate indirectly the acknowledgement of the PA of the gravity of VAW. In this context, it is important to institutionalise the monitoring, documentation and publication of updated data on VAW on a regular basis, to facilitate the development of appropriate and comprehensive intervention programmes and strategies by relevant stakeholders, including both CSOs and official institutions.

4.2 Constraints on and Challenges Facing Civil Society Organisations and Official Institutions

The number of CSOs in Palestine increased significantly after the establishment of the PA; they successfully assumed the role of a "watch dog" and scrutinised the adherence of the PA to human rights, lobbying it to fulfil its responsibilities. Similarly, the number of feminist CSOs increased; currently, there are more than 70 feminist organisations[44] working on the empowerment of Palestinian women. Several problematic aspects pervade the work of these organisations. A major one is that they do not perceive women's issues as societal issues that should be addressed by all stakeholders. This manifests in constricting work on feminist empowerment and gender equality to only feminist organisations, instead of societal organisations working on wider equality and empowerment issues.

---

[44]MoWA, *Feminist CSOs* (MoWA 2016) > http://www.mowa.pna.ps/etemplate.aspx?id=34>

The large number of feminist CSOs enabled them to focus on different aspects that oppress women; including the elimination of legal discrimination, addressing VAW, promoting economic empowerment and advancing political and civil participation. Despite the large number of CSOs, only limited breakthroughs were observed during the past two decades, as a direct result of minimal cooperation and consolidation of efforts through the adoption of unified national plans and strategies to empower women. More importantly, these CSOs vastly depend on international institutional donors to finance their programmes of intervention; this imposes restrictions on the types of programmes and activities they can set and implement.

Furthermore, in November 2003, the PA established that the MoWA would work strategically on empowering women in political participation, increase participation in the labour force, and reduce the frequency of all forms of VAW.[45] The budget of the MoWA within the national budget does not reach 1% of the 4.2 billion dollars annually.[46] In light of the limited budget of the MoWA, the ministry is currently competing with feminist CSOs for funding to be able to implement its programmes. In this context, the 'ghettoisation' or constriction of women's rights into a particular Ministry, instead of opting to mainstream gender issues and concerns throughout and across all other ministries, and the allocation of such a limited budget, raise serious concerns over the political will of the PA to take substantive steps to empower Palestinian women and to eliminate all forms of discrimination against them.

4.3 Complementary Strategies

Notwithstanding the significance of the aforementioned legal breakthroughs, they remain insufficient to ensure the protection of Palestinian women from violence and "honour" crimes. This requires transformation of the patriarchal framework that perceives

---

[45]MoWA, *Minister's Statement* (MoWA 2016) <http://www.mowa.pna.ps/etemplate.aspx?id=39>

[46]Ministry of Finance, *General Budget Law 2014* (Palestinian National Authority 2014) 374.

women as an auxiliary to men; by addressing the multitude of factors that inform and reinforce it, primarily a mentality of superiority and dominance. It is necessary in this case to implement a due diligence standard of intervention - where gender mainstreaming lies at its core. The due diligence standard consists of four main components: prevention, investigation, prosecution and compensation. The gender mainstreaming model referenced here identifies individual and systematic change on the formal and informal levels. For instance, legal reform falls in the systematic formal levels, while influencing cultural norms that underpin this vicious patriarchy lies in the informal systematic quarter.[47] Such work focusing on changing social norms and therefore gender stereotypes is crucial for the achievement of transformative equality; one of the most optimal methods in this context would include undertaking consolidated efforts towards the reform of the Palestinian educational system, including amendment of curriculum and rehabilitation of teachers and staff to not only breakdown gender stereotypes that are created and reinforced, but also actively mainstream human rights concepts and gender parity values.

Another important cornerstone, is the empowerment of women to enable them to report the different forms of violence, that they are subjected to, and equip them with the tools to counter and address them. An imperative to this end, is the economic empowerment of women to enable them to provide for themselves and their children, without needing to conform to familial hegemony and control. In light of the crippled Palestinian economy, and its dim prospects of advancement, one model towards the achievement of economic empowerment of women includes activating the social responsibility of the Palestinian private sector. The provision of microfinance and funding for income-generating projects, coupled with technical support of an entrepreneurial nature - particularly in terms of marketing and merchandising - would serve as the starting point for the realisation of such advancements. This model would create a win-win situation for both parties, where women would slowly progress towards economic independence, and the loan provider would become a shareholder in the

[47] Aruna Rao and David Kelleher, 'Is There Life After Gender Mainstreaming' (2010) Gender and Development 57, 60.

business; or would be repaid their loan after the project exceeds the break-even point, and is able to sustain itself.

Notwithstanding the disproportionate impact of violence on women, one could easily disregard the impact of the aforementioned framework of patriarchy and violence on the perpetrator. Within comprehensive interventions it is not only important to rehabilitate and reintegrate survivors of VAW but also engage perpetrators, instilling in them human rights concepts and citizenship values (most importantly equality). This entails the expansion of responsibilities and mandates of those entrusted with law enforcement. In this context, another civil society-led advocacy effort manifested in the drafting of the "Family Protection from Violence" law. The legislation serves as a precautionary measure to protect not only women, but also children from violence they are subjected to. One of the most important features of this draft law is that it shifts VAW from being a feminist issue into becoming a societal issue; where perpetrators are rehabilitated through capacity building trainings, awareness-raising workshops and hands-on training in the labour market to reintegrate them into the society. The enactment of such a law would be an acknowledgment of the adverse repercussions of patriarchy and masculinity not only on Palestinian women but also on Palestinian men, a major breakthrough that addresses social problems from their root causes.

On a more national policy level the 'ghettoisation' or constriction of women's issues into feminist organisations and MoWA, the fierce competition among CSOs and between CSOs and MoWA for funding and the predominant - almost exclusive - reliance on institutional donors is making the advancement of women's rights, and elimination of discrimination a very slow process. Comprehensively, several steps should be adopted including diversification of sources of funding of CSOs - including from the private sector, individual donors and income-generating projects and activities; this would enable them to address priority issues instead of conforming to the donor agenda.

Moreover, there is an urgent need to consolidate efforts and cooperation among CSOs, and with official institutions through the development of strategic and annual plans; these plans should be set within a framework that women's issues are societal issues - that all stakeholders contribute to addressing. As such, an advocacy component targeting decision makers is imperative to mainstream women's issues and concerns throughout and across all official institutions and ministries. This requires major changes in annulling the restriction of women's empowerment to one Ministry, and the allocation of such a limited budget to that Ministry. Mainstreaming women's issues across all relevant Ministries and bodies would certainly contribute towards efficiency and more importantly effectiveness and impact. This lobbying should also extend to include gender-sensitive and responsive budgeting. One important component of these plans should be to build on the ratification of 18 international human rights law and international humanitarian law conventions and treaties, including CEDAW, International Covenant on Civil and Political Rights and International Covenant on Economic, Social and Cultural Rights without reservations; as well as the issuance of a standing invitation to the HRC special procedures, lobbying the PA to ratify the optional protocols to strengthen prospects of access to justice through inquiries and communications.

Moreover, the vast majority of the General Comments and Recommendations of the CCPR, CESCR, and CEDAW were issued prior to the ratification of the PA, giving CSOs a vast scope of interpretation for the development of strategies and programmes, making use of all relevant legal provisions, including GC and GR.[48] The plans and strategies should utilise the framework of the due diligence standard - particularly its first component "prevent" - adopting measures to push for the advancement of transformative equality, through reform of the educational system; including the adjustment of the curriculum and rehabilitation of teachers and counsellors to mainstream gender parity and equality, in light of the complexity and interrelation of rights, particularly if several intersectional identities coincide.

---

[48]Despite the importance of all of the legal provisions, the following are the most relevant: CEDAW: articles 2, 5, 7, 8, 10, 11, 13, 15, 16; GR 12, 16, 17, 19, 21, 23, 25.
ICCPR: articles 2, 3, 6, 11, 14, 23, 26; GC 4, 6, 14, 18, 19, 27, 28, 32.
ICESCR: articles 2, 3, 6, 7, 13, 15; GC 10, 13, 16, 18, 19, 21, 22.

5. Conclusion

VAW is a pervasive phenomenon that is primarily informed on the global level by patriarchy and masculinity. However, its attribution only to patriarchy and masculinity is by itself an oversimplification of VAW, that would only constitute one further challenge in its elimination. Accordingly, VAW is further informed and reinforced by differing factors in differing contexts. VAW in Palestine extends beyond societal patriarchy and masculinity to include the role of the Israeli occupation, economic dynamics and stability, public/private divide in the legal system and the absence of alternatives.

On a different level, several official and non-governmental actors are working on addressing VAW in the Palestinian society. A critique of their strategy, includes limited consolidation of efforts, scarcity of resources, and constriction of the responsibility of gender equality to feminist actors, instead of mainstreaming these issues across all relevant bodies. Despite the many advancements by the aforementioned actors - particularly in terms of legal breakthroughs - they remain insufficient to eliminate VAW in Palestine. In order for that to happen, the causes that inform VAW should be addressed. Accordingly, there is a need for reform of the educational system, economic empowerment of women, and enactment of truly deterrent laws that clearly reflect the impermissibility of VAW.

WORKS CITED

Primary Sources

Legislation

2003 Amended Palestinian Basic Law

Jordanian Penal Code Number 16 of 1960

Ministry of Finance, *General Budget Law 2014* (Palestinian National Authority 2014)

Secondary Sources

Book Chapters

Coomaraswamy, R. 'Preface: Violence Against Women and "Crimes of Honour"' in L. Welchman and S. Hossain (eds.). *'Honour': Crimes, Paradigms, and Violence against Women.* Zed Books, 2005.

Idriss, M. M. 'Honour, Violence, Women and Islam—An Introduction' in M. M. Idriss and T. Abbas (eds.), *Honour, Violence, Women and Islam*. Routledge Taylor and Francis Group, 2011.

Mirza, H. S. and Meetoo, V. '"There Is Nothing 'Honourable' about Honour Killings": Gender, Violence and the Limits of Multiculturalism' in M. M. Idriss and T. Abbas (eds.), *Honour, Violence, Women and Islam.* Routledge Taylor and Francis Group, 2011.

Sarraj, S. 'Screaming in Silence' in Marguerite R. Waller and Jennifer Rycenga (eds.), *Frontline Feminisms: Women, War, and Resistance.* Taylor & Francis, 2001.

Singh, S. C. 'Gender Violence: Some Contextual Issues' in K Uma Devi (ed.), *Violence Against Women: Human Rights Perspective*. Serials Publications, 2005.

Touma-Sliman, A. 'Culture, National Minority, and the State: Working against the "Crimes of Honour" within the Palestinian Community in Israel' in L. Welchman and S. Hossain (eds.), *'Honour': Crimes, Paradigms, and Violence against Women.* Zed Books, 2005.

Welchman, L. and Hossain, S. 'Introduction: "Honour", Rights and Wrongs' in L. Welchmanand S. Hossain (eds.), *'Honour': Crimes, Paradigms, and Violence against Women.* Zed Books, 2005.

Books

Ahuja, R. *Violence Against Women*. Rawat Publications, 2003.

Hooks, B. *We Real Cool: Black Men and Masculinity*. Routledge: New York and London, 2004.

Misra, P. *Domestic Violence Against Women: Legal Control and Judicial Response*. Deep & Deep Publications 2007.

Women's Centre for Legal Aid and Counselling. *Right to Life Denied: Killing of Women in Palestine Social Reality and the Law 2011-2012*. Women's Centre for Legal Aid and Counselling, 2013.

Journal Articles

Charlesworth, H., Chinkin, C., and Wright, S. 'Feminist Approaches to International Law' (1991) 85 *American Journal of International Law* 613.

Pahl, J. 'Patterns of Money Management within Marriage' (1980) 9 *Journal of Social Policy* 313.

Rao, A. and Kelleher, D. 'Is There Life After Gender Mainstreaming' (2010) *Gender and Development* 57.

Welchman L, 'Honour and Violence Against Women in a Modern Shar'i Discourse' (2007) 5 *HAWWA*

United Nations Documents

Declaration on the Elimination of Violence Against Women (adopted 20 December 1993 UNGA Resolution 48/104).

Economic and Social Council, 'Report of the Special Rapporteur on Violence Against Women, its Causes and Consequences, Yakin Ertürk: Mission to Occupied Palestinian Territory' (2 February 2005) UN Doc E/CN.4/2005/72/Add.4 .

UN Committee for the Elimination of All Forms of Discrimination against Women, 'General Recommendation No 19' in 'Note by the Secretariat, Compilation of General Comments and General Recommendations Adopted by Human Rights Treaty Bodies' (29 July 1994) UN Doc HRI/GEN/1/Rev.1.

National Interviews, Statistics, and Studies

Interview with Soraida Abed Hussein, General Director of Women's Affairs Technical Committee (Ramallah, Palestine, 23 December 2015)

Women's Centre for Legal Aid and Counselling Documentation Reports on "Femicide" 2007-2015.

Women's Affairs Technical Committee, Gaps, Challenges and Opportunities in the Services System Provided to Women

Survivors of Gender Based Violence in the Gaza Strip Study (Alianza por la Solidaridad 2014)

Internet Sources

2011-2019 National Strategy to Combat Violence Against Women http://mowa.pna.ps/English%20Part.pdf.

General Secretariat of the Council of Ministers Third Quarterly Report http://www.palestinecabinet.gov.ps/WebSite/Upload/Documents/gov13_q1.pdf.

Ministry of Women's Affairs, Feminist CSOs (MoWA 2016) <http://www.mowa.pna.ps/etemplate.aspx?id=34>

Ministry of Women's Affairs, Minister's Statement (MoWA 2016) <http://www.mowa.pna.ps/etemplate.aspx?id=39>

Palestinian Central Bureau of Statistics, Palestine Statistical Yearbook 2014 <http://www.pcbs.gov.ps/Downloads/book2093.pdf>

Palestinian Central Bureau of Statistics, Violence in the Palestinian Society Survey 2011 <http://www.pcbs.gov.ps/Portals/_Rainbow/Documents/vio_a.htm>

Palestinian Central Bureau of Statistics, Women and Men in Palestine: Issues and Statistics 2014 <http://www.pcbs.gov.ps/Downloads/book2092.pdf>

Is Pornography Merely Obscene? Feminist Perspectives on the Regulation of Pornography

Godwin Tan[1]

Feminist legal theory strives, in part, to uncover the ways in which gender shapes law (and vice versa) and propose solutions to change or redirect the law to rectify gender inequality. In this sense, this is a feminist project focusing on the regulation of coercive heterosexual pornography. Traditionally, liberal states around the world, such as the United Kingdom, rely mainly on obscenity law to minimise the dissemination of pornography. However, such an approach is conceptually flawed and, in practice, it will continue to inadequately protect women who are harmed in and through pornography. This is because the traditional approach misunderstands the nature of the damage that flows from pornography and avoids expressly addressing a multitude of indirect harm. Instead, prominent radical feminists view pornography as not merely perversity but also a display and exercise of male dominance. In the light of this understanding, the radical feminist's approach is to expressly acknowledge that pornography is an issue of gender inequality, and one way to resolve this inequality is through an adjudicatory shift. Specifically, I argue in this paper that adjudication through a dominant/subordinate lens is a

[1]LLB candidate, University College London (UCL), and President of the UCL Law Society.

preferable alternative that the law and courts should adopt.

Keywords: Radical feminism, liberal feminism, pornography, obscenity law, criminal law, jurisprudence.

1. Introduction

Liberal states around the world, including the United Kingdom, aspire towards achieving civil liberties like freedom of speech and privacy, and regard themselves as neutral arbiters amongst conflicting interests in society.[2] From John Stuart Mill's fight for women's suffrage in the 19th century to more contemporary protests against genital mutilation in Sudan, liberal feminism has gained traction worldwide and is often seen as a source of empowerment for women.[3]

While recognising the contributions of liberal feminism, prominent radical feminists, such as Catharine MacKinnon and Andrea Dworkin, criticise liberal states for evading considerations of gender dynamics and dealing with specific issues of sexuality, such as rape, abortion and pornography, under categories of law that involve seemingly gender-neutral moral concerns.[4] They argue that liberal states mischaracterise such issues and fail to adequately empower and protect women in these areas.

In this paper, I focus on the issue of pornography and its implications on women. Concurring with radical feminists, I argue that the liberal state's traditional reliance on obscenity law to regulate pornography is conceptually flawed. I will first define pornography and set out the liberal state's position on pornography. I will then explicate the harm in and of pornography from the radical feminist's viewpoint, showing how the liberal state overlooks such harm. Finally, I will advocate an adjudicatory shift: pornography

[2]Catharine MacKinnon, *Toward a Feminist Theory of the State* (HUP 1989) 159. The term 'liberal state' was adopted from the works of radical feminists and the term is interchangeable with 'liberal nation'.
[3]Martha Nussbaum, *Sex and Social Justice* (OUP 1999) 55-58.
[4]MacKinnon, *Toward*, 159.

should be understood, by the courts, as an issue of gender inequality and expressly addressed through a dominant/subordinate model that will ultimately benefit women.

2. Definitions: Pornography and Liberal State

In 1997, MacKinnon and Dworkin defined pornography as the graphic, sexually explicit subordination of women, whether in pictures or in words.[5] This refers to a subset of explicit and coercive heterosexual materials that, in their view, should be civilly actionable. As my aim is to provide an exegesis of the radical feminist's position, I will mainly use this definition.[6]

There are many types of liberal states and schools of feminism, and a detailed discussion of the large range of types and their differences is beyond the scope of this paper. To outline the main liberal and radical feminist positions, I will focus on the descriptions of two prominent contributors in this field: Mill and MacKinnon, respectively. I will also substantiate these descriptions and my arguments with cases from the United Kingdom and the United States. Broadly speaking, there are two main features of the liberal state: negative liberty and formal equality.

Negative Liberty — In the liberal state, society is treated as a marketplace of ideas, and the freedom of expression is regarded as a fundamental right that serves the common good.[7] Free expression allows people to, *inter alia*, test their ideas, acquire new knowledge and develop more fully as human beings.[8] With this understanding, the liberal state focuses on maximising negative liberty: it strives towards ensuring that people are permitted to express themselves as they want and do as they please without

---

[5]Catharine MacKinnon and Andrea Dworkin (eds.), *In Harm's Way* (HUP 1997) 444.

[6]I address the problems with this definition below ('Feminist and amateur pornography').

[7]Erik Asard and Lance Bennett, *Marketplace of Ideas* (CUP 1997) 28.

[8]JS Mill, *On Liberty* (Hackett 1978) 16.

state interference, as long as they do not harm others.[9] Such harm is narrowly construed to mainly comprise interference to one's bodily integrity or the fear of such physical interference.[10]

Pornography is regarded as an exercise of free speech in the liberal state.[11] Therefore, to restrict pornography (i.e. infringe the liberty of another), one has to show that pornography is sufficiently harmful. If the harm in pornography is insufficient to displace this burden, the liberal state will not allow any interference with pornography. A famous instance of this balancing act is found in *American Booksellers Association v Hudnut*[12]. In this case, a group of distributors and readers of books, magazines and films argued that an ordinance prohibiting pornography is unconstitutional. The court held that the ordinance did contravene the First Amendment as it restrains the kinds of ideas that could be transmitted. The court thought that even if pornography does convey certain "wrong or even hateful" opinions and ideas this 'wrong', on its own, is not sufficiently harmful and will not justify regulation. Something further, such as obscenity (offending public decency) without value, is required to invoke state intervention.

Formal Equality — Liberal feminism adopts an Aristotelian conception of equality: treating likes alike and unlikes un-alike.[13] Equality is judged by proximity to the standards of the dominant group. In other words, the non-dominant group has to be "similarly situated" to the dominant group, and only then is there normative thrust to ground an equality claim.[14] For instance, in *Price Waterhouse v Hopkins*[15], a woman was found to have been discriminated against during a promotion cycle; the court found evidence of gender stereotyping during the employer's decision-making process. However, before she could establish this claim of

---

[9]Ibid, 9.

[10]Ibid.

[11]Ronald Dworkin, 'Women and Pornography' (1993) *NY Review* 39.

[12]American Booksellers Association v Hudnut, 771 F 2d 323 (1985).

[13]William Ross (transl.), *Aristotle: Nicomachean Ethics* (Lesley Brown ed., OUP 2009) 142-162.

[14]Catharine MacKinnon, 'Reflections on Sex Equality' (1991) 100 YLJ 1281,1297.

[15]490 US 228 (1989).

gender discrimination, she had to first prove that she was doing work that is substantively equivalent to that of her male colleagues. While at first blush this promotes formal equality, in truth, it has the potential to conceal substantive inequality. Specifically, the liberal state does not question why such standards are used to measure both men and women and to whose favour.[16] At all times, the liberal state claims to be 'neutral': women are treated as abstract persons with abstract rights, taking no account of the social foundations and disadvantages of their gender.[17] Only the few women who could, against the odds, be similarly situated with men are entitled to equal treatment. In other words, under this sameness/difference paradigm, other women - the less wealthy and educated, but more vulnerable to abuse - tend to fall off the equality map.

Furthermore, the liberal state, with its strong focus on sameness to establish equality, has difficulties accommodating issues of sexuality. Violations through rape and pornography are regarded as chiefly female experiences with hardly any equivalent male yardstick, meaning no like cases to treat alike.[18] Partly as a consequence of this, such issues are excluded from equality and discrimination laws and instead dealt with under other areas of law. For instance, pornography is dealt with in English law mainly under the Obscene Publications Act 1959, as amended by the Obscene Publications Act 1964, and the Criminal Justice and Immigration Act (CJIA) 2008.[19] Obscenity law is designed to penalise purveyors and prevent obscene articles from reaching the market

---

[16]MacKinnon, *Reflections*, 1292.

[17]MacKinnon, *Toward*, 160.

[18]Ibid, 243. Men who are raped are acknowledged in the liberal state but are regarded, statistically and socially, as exceptions rather than the norm.

[19]The CJIA only covers images that are "grossly offensive, disgusting or otherwise of an obscene nature" (s 63(6)(b)). Therefore, I will discuss it as a part of the general obscenity legislation. The Digital Economy Bill 2016-17 is at the time of writing debated in the House of Lords and will not be dealt with in this paper.

and offending public decency.[20] Specifically, it controls how much and what kind of sex can be publicly seen by people.[21]

Prima facie, this sends a strong message against pornography, but on a closer examination, categorising pornography as an obscene publication is problematic because of the nature of the harm in pornography.

3. Pornography and Harm

3.1 Overview

Radical feminists believe that coercive heterosexual pornography is and causes harm to women. Its influence is both physical and psychological, and its long-term effects are *social*. It is clear that direct harm is sometimes inflicted on pornographic actresses during the making of pornography.[22] Furthermore, MacKinnon argues that there is indirect harm to women as a group that the liberal state fails to recognise.[23]

I suggest that such indirect harm is partly possible because women used in pornography are *used* in pornography *as women*. This is evident in that most women in pornography are nameless or given pseudonyms, and deliberately conform in likeness and mannerism to gender and cultural stereotypes (for instance, the hypersexualised shy schoolgirl).[24] Women, but not men, are also customarily cast into genres based on their age or nationality to cater to the preferences of the viewer.[25] Through such methods, pornography ensures that women are unacknowledged as individual beings but immediately recognisable as a violable group.

---

[20] *R v Smith* [2012] EWCA Crim 398, [2012] 1 WLR 3368.

[21] MacKinnon, *Toward*, 200.

[22] MacKinnon, *In*, 44-199.

[23] I adopt Eaton's language of "direct/indirect harm" – Anne Eaton, 'Sensible Antiporn Feminism' (2007) *Ethics Journal* 674, 677.

[24] Celine Shimizu, *Hypersexuality of Race* (DUP 2007) 165.

[25] Linda Williams, Hard Core: Power, Pleasure, and Frenzy of the Visible (UCP 1999) 87.

This encourages a new way of seeing women in society, bringing the harm of pornography outside of the realm of the individual and into that of the collective.[26]

With this understanding, I specify three heads of indirect harm that flow from pornography, noting that this is not an exhaustive list.[27] They are, namely, the eroticisation of male aggression, the dehumanisation of women and the sustenance of the gender hierarchy. These heads of indirect harm are distinct from the liberal state's concerns of obscenity, and I shall discuss them in order even though in reality they may at times overlap:

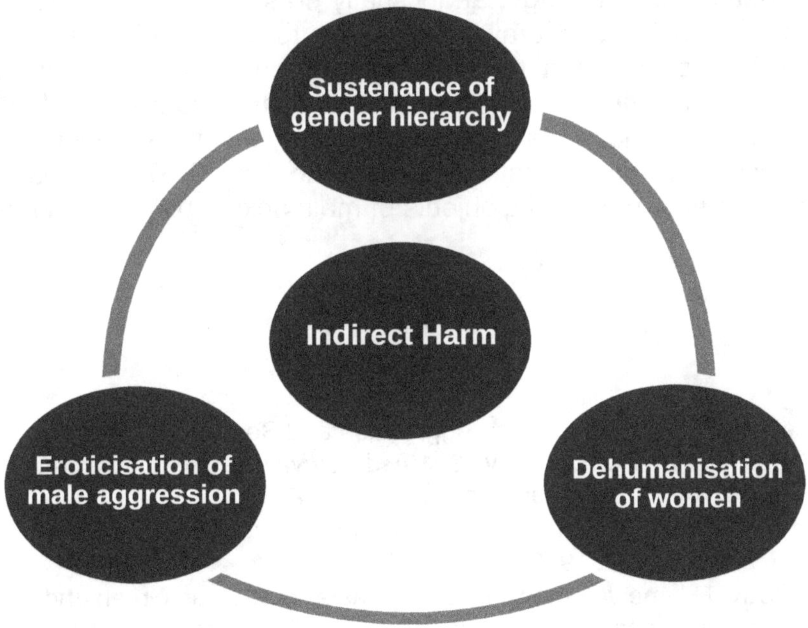

Eroticisation of Male Aggression. At the outset, pornography tends to eroticise male aggression and the violation of women. In pornography, male aggression often elicits strong positive re-

[26]Catharine MacKinnon, *Feminism Unmodified* (HUP 1987) 130.
[27]For other heads – Gary Brooks, *Centerfold Syndrome* (JBP 1995).

sponses from women.[28] Even when women do appear to be in distress, their humiliation is presented as entertaining and sexually arousing.[29] Through such means, pornography endorses women's subordination and distorts the ethical understanding of the viewer by training his or her emotions to respond positively towards gender inequality and "perverting the sentiments of the heart."[30] The viewer is conditioned to have a "physiologically real conviction" that male sexual aggression is to be celebrated.[31]

Dehumanisation of Women. Pornography dehumanises women in two ways. First, pornography objectifies and encourages the objectification of women. Women are often described in fetishistic and patriarchal language, and visually presented in unnatural positions exposing and drawing attention to their genitals.[32] Laura Mulvey suggests that by reducing women to their body parts, pornography encourages men to adopt, and women to identify with, the male gaze, namely a critically voyeuristic, fetishistic, illusionistic and representational way of looking.[33] This urges the viewer to treat women as objects of male sexual pleasure, a mere

---

[28]Ana Bridges and others, 'Aggression and Sexual Behaviour in Best-Selling Pornography' (2010) <http://vaw.sagepub.com/content/16/10/1065.full.pdf> accessed 20 March 2016.

[29]Shimizu, 176; Gloria Steinem, *Outrageous Acts and Everyday Rebellions* (NAL 1983) 241.

[30]David Hume, 'Of the Standard of Taste' in Thomas Green and Thomas Grose (eds), *Essays: Moral, Political, and Literary* (LF 1985).

[31]MacKinnon, *In*, 312; empirically supported – Dolf Zillmann and Jennings Bryant, 'Effects of Massive Exposure to Pornography' in Neil Malamuth and Edward Donnerstein (eds), *Pornography and Sexual Aggression* (AP 1984); Dolf Zillmann, *Connections Between Sexuality and Aggression* (PP 1998).

[32]Shimizu, *Hypersexuality*, 235; Williams, *Hard*, 72.

[33]Laura Mulvey, 'Visual Pleasure and Narrative Cinema' in Leo Braudy and Marshall Cohen (eds), *Film Theory and Criticism* (OUP 1999).

means to an end, contravening Kant's humanity formulation.[34] While Martha Nussbaum argues that "Lawrentian objectification" (temporary objectification between lovers) is good as it enhances the sexual experience,[35] in the context of pornography, the objectification is often deliberately degrading and disrespectful to the woman.[36] This context stains the meaning and value of the objectification.

Second, radical feminists argue that pornography dehumanises women by eroticising that which is not human. Humans tend to seek pleasure,[37] but women are presented as craving pain in positions of extreme vulnerability.[38] Humans tend to want autonomy and self-determination,[39] but women are shown to desire full servility to degrading male orders, abandoning all bodily integrity. By presenting all women as being *eager* to be violated and *only* to be violated, pornography constructs a womanhood that lacks the semblance of personhood.

Sustenance of Gender Hierarchy. Lastly, pornography is not just a manifestation of male power. It also has the perlocutionary effect of reinforcing women's subordinate social status, effectively promoting and sustaining the patriarchal social order. By making abuses of power asymmetries appear pervasive and libidinally enjoyable for men and women, pornography incentivises society to sustain the gender hierarchy. It also presents this power imbal-

---

[34]In a nutshell, Kant's humanity formula states that we should never treat ourselves or others as a mere means to an end. The merits of Kant's humanity formula are beyond this paper. Robert Johnson, 'Kant's Moral Philosophy', *The Stanford Encyclopedia of Philosophy* (Summer edition, 2014) <http://plato.stanford.edu/entries/kant-moral/ > accessed 21 March 2016.

[35]Nussbaum, *Sex*, 251.

[36]Shimizu, *Hypersexuality*, 178.

[37]Besides being an everyday observation, this is a key pillar of Bentham's utilitarianism. Jeremy Bentham, *Principles of Morals and Legislation* (CP 1907).

[38]To be clear, there are, in reality, men and women who actively seek out sadomasochistic sexual practices. This means that the pain/pleasure distinction could have furry edges, and this is discussed in greater detail below (see 'The Liberated Woman').

[39]This is "at the heart of Kant's moral theory." Johnson, *Kant's*, 1.

ance as the way things are and how they should remain. This notion, once accepted, makes power and powerlessness "invisible as harm."[40]

3.2 Addressing Objections: Questioning the Harm

Such indirect harm is either overlooked or downplayed in the liberal state. First, several academics and researchers have argued that pornography is merely fantasy, namely that there is no indirect harm at all. Alternatively, they have argued that there is no evidence indicating that pornography leads to people directly harming others. I contend that both views are flawed. By adopting an overly narrow conception of harm, the liberal state fails to see gender politics in pornography and thereby misunderstands the problem.

3.3 Merely Fantasy?

For instance, Laura Kipnis argues that pornography is just "male fantasy", meaning merely symbolic and causing no indirect harm. [41] However, MacKinnon argues that pornography not only reveals "what men want", it is a "mirror of reality" reflecting everyday sexual intercourse even when the cameras are off. [42] MacKinnon premises this view on, inter alia, the assumption that dominance is an "imperative…of masculinity."[43]

In my view, neither side is particularly persuasive on this issue. MacKinnon does not explain the origins of such a desire to dominate women: is it inherent (i.e. pre-social), and how can we really tell?[44] Her view is weakened by the fact that sexually explicit films that portray mutually respecting parties are capable of arousing

[40]MacKinnon, *Toward*, 204.

[41]Laura Kipnis, Bound and Gagged: Pornography and the Politics of Fantasy (DUP 1998) 158.

[42]MacKinnon, *Toward*, 138, 197-198.

[43]Ibid, 130.

[44]Katherine Bartlett, 'MacKinnon's Feminism: Power on Whose Terms?' (1987) 75 *California LR* 1559.

men.[45] In fact, some men regard acts featuring male dominance/female subordination as sexually repelling.[46] These indicate that dominance may not be an essential component of male sexuality. From this view, MacKinnon's understanding of sexuality lacks a fully explained genesis and runs the risk of hasty generalisation.[47] Pornography, then, may well be the fantasy of the corrupt.

However, even if Kipnis is right about pornography being a fantasy, this is not the crux of the matter. It is important to note that even "fantasy expresses ideology."[48] Metaphysically, pornography is "sadism… which ritually [murders] a part of women in both body and mind."[49] Representationally, pornography hyperbolises female sexual availability, endorses male supremacy, and distorts social understanding of sexual roles and norms to the detriment of women.[50] In short, projecting and endorsing what is essentially guiltless rape over and over again, even as fantasy, can and does harm.

3.4 Evidence of Harm?

Is there evidence of this harm? Berl Kutchinsky's studies suggest that MacKinnon's concerns are mere possibilities that have no grounding in reality – "the link between [pornography and rape] is more than weak."[51] Similarly, David van Mill notes that even with

---

[45]Tristan Taormino and others, *Feminist Porn Book* (FP 2013).

[46]Shimizu, *Hypersexuality*, 177-179.

[47]Notwithstanding MacKinnon's lack of explanation, I note that the more crucial issue is that men are encouraged or expected to be aroused by pornography depicting male dominance/female subordination.

[48]MacKinnon, *Toward*, 198.

[49]Susan Griffith, *Pornography and Silence* (HarperCollins 1981) 83.

[50]Covenant Eyes, 'Pornography Statistics' (2015) <http://www.covenanteyes.com/lemonade/wp-content/uploads/2013/02/2015-porn-stats-covenant-eyes.pdf> accessed 21 March 2016.

[51]Berl Kutchinsky, 'Pornography and Rape: Theory and Practice?' (1991) <http://www.sciencedirect.com/science/article/pii/016025279190024H> accessed 21 March 2016.

the "explosion of pornography on the Internet," there has been no significant increase in sexual offences and physical abuse against women.[52] If so, the liberal state has not misunderstood the harm in pornography. The harm is merely obscenity, and claims of other types of harm are merely alarmist.

To begin, MacKinnon contends that attempting to prove or disprove the harm in pornography through a positivistic, linear causation test misses the point.[53] This is true insofar as the harm in pornography operates through influencing attitudes within the social system and has facets that cannot be isolated to rape statistics alone (eg objectification, dehumanisation etc).

Nevertheless, in my view, radical feminists are still challenged to provide at least some form of empirical justification. Defending MacKinnon's position, I submit that empirical evidence is at best polarised. Much ink has been spilled on this battleground. There are studies indicating that pornography contributes to a positive attitude towards non-consensual intercourse, and encourages heterosexual men to desire "bizarre" and "hardcore" sexual encounters with women.[54] Contrary studies are also rife with methodological fallacies, such as the tendency to exclude unreported sexual offences.[55] In the UK alone, around 85 per cent of serious sexual offences (female victims) are not reported to the police.[56] Therefore, conclusions pointing to a definite absence of correlation and causation between pornography and sexual offences remain questionable at best.

---

[52]David van Mill, 'Freedom of Speech', *The Stanford Encyclopedia of Philosophy* (Spring edition 2015) <http://plato.stanford.edu/entries/freedom-speech/> accessed 21 March 2016.

[53]MacKinnon, *Toward*, 207.

[54]Jill Manning, 'Impact of Internet Pornography on Marriage and the Family' (2005) <s3.amazonaws.com/thf_media/2010/pdf/ManningTST.pdf> accessed 21 March 2016; Anthony Mulac, Laura Jansma, and Daniel Linz, 'Men's Behavior toward Women after Viewing Sexually-Explicit Films' (2002) *Communication Monographs* 311.

[55]Eaton, *Sensible*, 699.

[56]Ministry of Justice, 'Overview of Sexual Offending' (2013) <https://www.gov.uk/government/statistics/an-overview-of-sexual-offending-in-england-and-wales> accessed 22 March 2016.

Furthermore, with greater consumption of pornography, the viewer of pornography becomes increasingly desensitised to force before and during intercourse.[57] This has shaped sexual norms and normalised a higher degree of force within what is socially regarded as 'consensual sex'.[58] Such norms spill over into the legal realm as, in many jurisdictions, the test for rape hinges on the man's *mens rea*: did he have a reasonable belief that the other person consented (e.g. Sexual Offences Act 2003, s 1(1)(c))? Since the reasonable man now has a higher threshold when it comes to the 'permissible' level of force before and during sexual intercourse, it is more difficult for women to prove that the *act* of rape was actually the *crime* of rape despite being violated. From this view, when "men coerce women, women 'consent'."[59]

4. Misunderstanding Pornography

Through explicating the harm in pornography, radical feminists deconstruct gender and sexuality as androcentric, exposing pornography as a product of male power and a channel through which misogynistic behaviours are normalised and celebrated. Male dominance, then, is the problem. This understanding is key in showing that the liberal state's regulation of pornography is misguided. Its regulatory methods, as described previously, simply do not address the issue at its core.

4.1 Freedom of Speech and Marketplace of Ideas

As mentioned, the liberal state aims at maximising negative freedom, and this is reflected in its approach to pornography. In the public sphere, freedom of speech trumps equality interests, unless there is sufficient harm to justify limiting such speech. The

---

[57] Neil Malamuth and Joseph Ceniti, 'Repeated Exposure to Violent and Nonviolent Pornography' (1986) <www.sscnet.ucla.edu/comm/malamuth/pdf/86ab12.pdf> accessed 22 March 2016.

[58] Rae Langton, *Sexual Solipsism* (OUP 2009) 2-3.

[59] MacKinnon, *Toward*, 168.

liberal state accounts for its largely *laissez-faire* approach on the basis that it is giving *both* men and women the (negative) freedom to express themselves without impediment and accordingly, "flourish [...] in the marketplace of ideas."[60] The precise contribution of pornography, especially coercive and brutal ones, to 'human flourishing' and the 'marketplace of ideas' is questionable.[61] As Dworkin writes, "When a woman has a penis thrust down to the bottom of her throat... that throat is not discussing ideas."[62] That woman is not flourishing.

Furthermore, the liberal state's justification only works if, looking broadly at legal, cultural, social, emotional and financial pressures, men and women have equal power against each other. This is not true in most contemporary societies, where many women still remain 'weaker' than men. MacKinnon highlights the historical fact that modern legal regimes and governing systems were designed and presided by powerful men ("no woman had a voice").[63] She argues that this leads to an androcentric social system that protects and projects male power. Mill had a similar sentiment and warned that the patriarchy was wrong for subordinating women.[64] To me, while it is difficult to prove that just because no woman had a voice in designing society, society must be male-centric, chances are that female concerns have been excluded intentionally or otherwise. Since women have been silenced through the social system and its conditioning, no matter how much freedom of speech is given to women legally, they will fail to meaningfully exercise their speech in practice.[65] The liberal state, by evading concerns of gender dynamics, overlooks this possibility, and its 'negative liberty' model ultimately favours the male voice over the female one.

---

[60] Shaun Young, *Analysis of Political Liberalism* (UPA 2002); Ronald Dworkin, 'Is There a Right to Pornography?' (1981) *OJLS* 177, 178.

[61] Andrea Dworkin, 'Pornography Happens to Women' (1993) <http://www.nostatusquo.com/ACLU/dworkin/PornHappens.html> accessed on 3 April 2016.

[62] Ibid.

[63] MacKinnon, *Reflections*, 1282.

[64] JS Mill, *Subjection of Women* (Hackett 1988) 261.

[65] MacKinnon, *Toward*, 164.

4.2 Obscenity Law

The liberal state's use of obscenity law to regulate pornography also reflects a failure to understand the harm in pornography. Under obscenity law, pornography is harmful because it "depraves and corrupts" those whose minds are susceptible to such influences.[66] Obscenity law is concerned with moral purity, assessed against communal standards of public decency.[67] The use of such language to describe pornography is also mirrored in other jurisdictions, reflecting its prevalence.[68]

The liberal state does not confront pornography as an issue of male dominance *qua* dominance. Under obscenity law, dehumanisation and degradation of women are not problems *per se*. Obscenity law is concerned solely with the potential corruption of the viewer (overwhelmingly men).[69] The interests of the subject in pornography and victims of its indirect harm (overwhelmingly women) are absent from legal considerations.[70] Therefore, the liberal state "cares more about whether men blush than whether women bleed."[71] By eschewing considerations of gender, the liberal state privileges the subordination of women. Gender inequality becomes shielded, and the notion that women are subhumans that yearn for sexual exploitation is condoned. By treating pornography as a gender-neutral conflict between the right to free speech and public morality, the liberal state erroneously disregards the unequal power dynamics within and beyond pornography.

Not only is obscenity conceptually distinct from the aforementioned indirect harm (dehumanisation, sustenance of gender hierarchy etc), this labelling also makes a practical difference. Communal standards are malleable and imprecise. How obscene

[66] *R v Hicklin* (1867–8) LR 3 QB 360, as seen in *R v Smith* [2012] EWCA Crim 398, [2012] 1 WLR 3368.

[67] Catharine MacKinnon, 'Not a Moral Issue' (1984) 2 *Yale LPR* 321, 323.

[68] Undesirable Publications Act (Chapter 338) in Singapore and *Miller v California*, 413 U.S. 15 (1973).

[69] Eyes, *Pornography*, 17-20.

[70] Ibid.

[71] Catharine MacKinnon, *Are Women Human?* (HUP 2007) 113.

must a pornographic scene be in order to be *considered* as obscene *by society*? In an androcentric social order, 'communal standards' favour the male standpoint.[72] Recent application of obscenity law reflects a greater tolerance for male sexual dominance. Male acts of fisting, urolagnia and electrical torture have all been excluded from the obscenity label.[73] As Kennedy writes, "law does not spring out of a social vacuum."[74] In a male-centric society, it is my view that obscenity law cannot be relied on to adequately address the harm in pornography.

4.3 Public/Private Divide

This problem is exacerbated as the liberal state refrains from intervening in the "private sphere" (notoriously difficult to define but it usually refers to the family home), as it aspires to respect individual autonomy and privacy.[75] This supposedly *a priori* private/public split is arguably a man-made political arrangement, and its very existence works against women.[76] In an androcentric society, whose privacy is actually protected? By not interfering in the 'private', the liberal state legitimises power asymmetries where women are most vulnerable to male dominance. Men become mostly unaccountable, and epistemologically male dominance is once again obscured.[77] Instead of empowering women to flourish, the message here is, "do anything to women with impunity in pri-

[72]"I know it when I see it", *per* Judge Stewart in Jacobellis v Ohio, 378 US 184 (1964).

[73]*R v Peacock* - Unreported, 6 January 2011 (Crown Court, Southwark). Discussed here - <http://www.lawgazette.co.uk/analysis/obscenity-trial-shows-up-outdated-law/63682.fullarticle> accessed 3 April 2016.

[74]Helena Kennedy, *Eve was Framed* (Vintage 1993) 17.

[75]David Dyzenhaus, 'Mill and Harm of Pornography' (1992) *Ethics Journal* 534, 535.

[76]MacKinnon, *Toward*, 95.

[77]Ibid, 191.

vate."[78] In the private sphere, "we do not even have sling shots against Goliath."[79]

From a radical feminist standpoint, the liberal state misunderstands pornography as a gender-neutral issue of public morality. The 'objective' moral norms of the liberal state–freedom of expression and privacy–are revealed as androcentric epistemology. Such norms silence women's concerns of objectification, dehumanisation and domination. Pornography is, in fact, a political reality (male power and female powerlessness) that forcefully towers over the female standpoint. While the liberal state shuns from this revelation, a shift to assessing pornography under MacKinnon's dominant/subordinate model confronts the problem. From an adjudicative point of view, courts that are awaken to the power dynamics and relations between the genders will be able to intervene where men are overly dominant and women are overly subordinate.

If systemic inequality and sexual abuse cannot outweigh the right to free expression, then such civil liberties become weapons used to "bludgeon [unarmed] women."[80] By treating pornography as a gender equality issue, not as an issue of free speech or privacy, the state will more adequately protect women in both the public and private.

5. Is it Preferable to Shift to a Dominant/ Subordinate Dyadic?

However, I anticipate one major objection against shifting to a dominant/subordinate dyadic. This objection would be raised by women who claim to have a *bona fide* desire to be in a subordinate position. In reality, the distinctions between pain/pleasure and dominant/subordinate may have furry edges and respecting diversity in female experiences makes it necessary to address the concerns of these women.

---

[78]Ibid.

[79]MacKinnon, *In*, 319.

[80]Ibid.

5.1 The Liberated Woman

It has been suggested that some women genuinely desire subordination. Liberal feminists argue that radical feminists, in their assumption that powerlessness and subordination are irrefutably bad, fail to respect plurality in female preferences. Joshua Cohen argues that we must respect women's right to individual sexual autonomy and expression, even if this includes a desire to be dominated by men.[81] Nussbaum cautions that we should not assume that only loving sex is required for human flourishing.[82] Ostensibly, male domination/female subordination can be a legitimate expression deserving protection. The liberal state defends itself by claiming that radical feminists are the ones who misunderstand pornography.

But the underlying belief, here, is that men and women are generally able to choose equally freely; that the autonomy to determine one's sexual acts is on parity. *Per* Judge Barker in *American Booksellers*, women "have the capacity to protect themselves," freely choosing to participate in pornography.[83] Refuting this, MacKinnon contends that the notion that women have equal power to negotiate with men is a figment of the imagination, stripped of any understanding of the socio-economic constraints that women face.[84] As the poet Carol Ann Duffy writes in *Standing Female Nude*, "He is concerned with volume, space/ I with the next meal."[85] If so, the liberal state and liberal feminists are turning a blind eye to the plight of disenfranchised women.

However, pornographic actresses from wealthy or educated backgrounds have claimed that they chose the job out of desire, namely the "beauty, glamour and seduction."[86] Grace Quek, a gender studies graduate who starred in the *World's Biggest Gangbang* famously said that she enjoyed being treated "like a

---

[81]Joshua Cohen, 'Freedom, Equality and Pornography' in Jessica Spector (ed), *Prostitution and Pornography* (SUP 1996) 261.

[82]Nussbaum, *Sex*, 18-20.

[83]*American*, 771 F 2d 323 (1985).

[84]MacKinnon, *Toward*, 150.

[85]Carol Ann Duffy, *Standing Female Nude* (APP 1998).

[86]Shimizu, *Hypersexuality*, 37.

piece of meat."[87] Similarly, women in the BDSM community assert that their desire for bondage and submission is an "authentic personal interest."[88] While MacKinnon invokes the possibility of false consciousness (to MacKinnon, "I chose it" is merely the woman's "strategy for sanity"),[89] liberal feminists charge her with infantilising women.[90] As pornography becomes construed as a genuine preference, further intervention based on gender equality is unjustified bigotry and "thought control".[91]

To me, these liberal arguments are strong. While radical feminists rightly expose the artificiality of liberal personhood in that not all persons are equally free agents, they risk condescending to sex workers and denying diversity in female experiences. It is plausible that some women have meaningful agency and a *bona fide*, meaning non-socially conditioned, desire to be sexually subordinate.

However, while it is true that radical feminists do, in theory, make bold assumptions that may undermine female diversity, I suggest that MacKinnon's dominant/subordinate model could, in practice, accommodate such diversity in women's experiences. The dominant/subordinate model of gender equality provides a potential gateway to legal protection, where none under the liberal state exists. For instance, in *Carr v Allison Gas Turbine Division*[92], Carr's male colleagues made aggressive sexual gestures and used derogatory sexual remarks towards her; she retorted with the same. Descriptively, they did similar things. Judge Posner, overruling the lower court, found that the men were sexually ha-

---

[87]Ibid, 178.

[88]Backlash, 'Written Evidence' (2016) <http://data.parliament.uk/writtenevidence/committeeevidence.svc/evidencedocument/home-affairs-committee/prostitution/written/29058.html> accessed 22 March 2016.

[89]MacKinnon, *Toward*, 149.

[90]Jessica Elliott, *Role of Consent in Human Trafficking* (Routledge 2014) 111.

[91]*Per* Judge Easterbrook in *American*; Geoffrey Stone, 'Government must Leave to the People the Evaluation of Ideas' (2010) 77 *CLR* 1219.

[92]32 F 3d 1007 (1994).

rassing her, and this finding was only possible with an awareness of the power asymmetry between the genders.[93] The men (the powerful) were targeting her because of her femaleness, and she (the powerless) was merely defending herself.[94] Once female epistemic subjectivity is included within mainstream epistemology, courts become awakened to the actual social meaning of words and acts. Gender equality can then be invoked to protect the powerless *where necessary*.

Applied to pornography, (1) if a woman in pornography truly wants to express herself in that way, the court has discretion to not intervene. (2) If the woman was actually victimised, the court can intervene.[95] Based on the liberal state's erroneous conception of personhood, the liberated woman in (1) is assumed and the victimised woman in (2) is precluded. MacKinnon's dominant/subordinate dyadic is therefore still more effective than the liberal state in addressing the harm in pornography. In practical terms, this model would be incorporated in the adjudication process either by widening interpretations of equality laws or widening the definition of obscenity to include gender inequality as expressed in pornography.

5.2 Feminist and Amateur Pornography

As a final and more general criticism, the radical feminist's definition of pornography (above) is problematic in two ways. First, it assumes what it has to prove – that women are subordinated in pornography.[96] Second, key radical feminist texts such as *Toward a Feminist Theory of the State* were published before the Internet

[93]Ibid, 1009-1011. He said that the lower court failed to consider the "asymmetry of positions."

[94]Ibid, 1011.

[95]This requires accepting that at least some women cannot adequately protect themselves. Otherwise, this discretion will not be exercised, eg *American*.

[96]However, it is widely accepted that subordination exists in at least some pornography – Stephen Kershnar, *Sex, Discrimination and Violence* (UPA 2009) 34; Peter Lehman, *Pornography* (RUP 2006) 255.

revolution, at a time when the types of pornography were highly limited.[97] Such texts do not account for the wide range of feminist and amateur pornography that only increased in numbers since the 1990s.[98] Such pornography often depicts mutuality and clear consent.[99] For instance, in feminist pornography, camera angles deliberately avoid projecting misogynistic perspectives.[100] Similarly, in most amateur pornography, dialogue and acts between the sexes reflect balanced power dynamics, subverting the "desultory dominance" in "violation pornography."[101] The radical feminist's insights about the sexualisation of dominance, while compelling, mainly apply to coercive heterosexual pornography. The liberal state's failings are likewise limited to that genre.

6. Conclusion: Feminist insight and future developments

The purpose of this paper has been to expose the flaws in the traditional methods of regulating coercive heterosexual pornography and to advocate adjudication that properly addresses the harm in and of such pornography. I have argued that the liberal state's positions on freedom of speech and privacy are, in practice, disadvantageous to women and generally framed, intentionally or otherwise, in favour of men. Likewise, its use of obscenity law fails to address the many distinct heads of indirect harm, such as the objectification and dehumanisation of women.

---

[97]Richard Corliss, 'When Porno was Chic' (2005) <http://content.time.com/time/arts/article/0,8599,1043267,00.html> accessed 21 March 2016.

[98]Rebecca Sullivan and Alan McKee, *Pornography* (PP 2015) 162-166; Tristan Taormino, 'What is Feminist Porn?' (2013) <http://www.cosmopolitan.com/sex-love/news/a16343/tristan-taormino-feminist-porn-interview/> accessed 22 March 2016; Taormino, *Feminist*.

[99]Ibid

[100]Sullivan, *Pornography*.

[101]Kershnar, *Sex*; Lehman, *Pornography*.

There is therefore a need to demand that the liberal state gives a voice to the harmed women in and beyond pornography. In this paper, pornography is revealed as male power: it encourages and conceals female powerlessness and in turn sustains the gender hierarchy. This is what the liberal state fails to recognise. This is the male-female imbalance that it fails to redress. Coercive heterosexual pornography, then, is not merely obscene.

By ignoring power asymmetries between the genders, the liberal state fundamentally mischaracterises the nature of the harm involved. So long as it continues relying on a sameness/difference paradigm and 'gender-neutral' moral norms to approach issues of sexuality, the liberal state will be fundamentally limited in its march towards meaningful gender equality. In my view, a shift towards adjudication which specifically addresses pornography as an issue of male dominance vis-à-vis female subordination will benefit women.

Works Cited

Primary Sources

Legislation

Criminal Justice and Immigration Act 2008
Obscene Publications Act 1959.
Obscene Publications Act 1964.
Sexual Offences Act 2003.
Undesirable Publications Act (Chapter 338).

Case Law

American Booksellers Association v Hudnut, 771 F 2d 323 (1985).
Carr v Allison Gas Turbine Division, 32 F 3d 1007 (1994).
Jacobellis v Ohio, 378 US 184 (1964).
Miller v California, 413 US 15 (1973).
Price Water v Hopkins, 490 US 228 (1989).
R v Hicklin (1867–8) LR 3 QB 360.
R v Peacock (Unreported, 6 January 2011).

R v Smith [2012] EWCA Crim 398, [2012] 1 WLR 3368.

Reports

Bridges A, Robert Wosnitzer, Erica Scharrer, Chyng Sun and Rachael Liberman, 'Aggression and Sexual Behaviour in Best-Selling Pornography Videos' (2010) <http://vaw.sagepub.com/content/16/10/1065.full.pdf> accessed 20 March 2016.

Justice M, Home Office, and the Office for National Statistics, 'An Overview of Sexual Offending in England and Wales' (2013) <https://www.gov.uk/government/statistics/an-overview-of-sexual-offending-in-england-and-wales> accessed 22 March 2016.

Kutchinsky B, 'Pornography and Rape: Theory and Practice?' (1991) <http://www.sciencedirect.com/science/article/pii/016025279190024H> accessed 21 March 2016.

Malamuth N and Joseph Ceniti, 'Repeated Exposure to Violent and Nonviolent Pornography' (1986) <www.sscnet.ucla.edu/comm/malamuth/pdf/86ab12.pdf> accessed 22 March 2016.

Mulac A, Laura Jansma, and Daniel Linz, 'Men's Behavior toward Women after Viewing Sexually-Explicit Films' (2002) *Communication Monographs* 311.

Zillmann D and Jennings Bryant, 'Effects of Massive Exposure to Pornography' in Neil M Malamuth and Edward Donnerstein (eds), *Pornography and Sexual Aggression* (Academic Press 1984).

Secondary Sources

Books

Asard E and Bennett L, *Democracy and the Marketplace of Ideas* (Cambridge University Press 1997).

Bentham J, *Introduction to the Principles of Morals and Legislation* (Clarendon Press 1907).

Brooks G, *The Centerfold Syndrome* (Jossey-Bass Publications 1995).

Cohen J, 'Freedom, Equality and Pornography' in Jessica Spector (ed), *Prostitution and Pornography: Philosophical Debate about the Sex Industry* (Stanford University Press 1996).

Duffy C A, *Standing Female Nude* (Anvil Press Poetry 1998).

Elliott J, *The Role of Consent in Human Trafficking* (Routledge 2014).

Griffith S, *Pornography and Silence: Culture's Revenge Against Nature* (HarperCollins 1981).

Hume D, 'Of the Standard of Taste' in Thomas Hill Green and Thomas Hodge Grose (eds), *Essays Moral, Political, and Literary* (Liberty Fund 1985).

Kennedy H, *Eve was Framed: Women and British Justice* (Vintage 1993).

Kershnar S, *Sex, Discrimination and Violence: Surprising and Unpopular Results in Applied Ethics* (University Press of America 2009).

Kipnis L, *Bound and Gagged: Pornography and the Politics of Fantasy in America* (Duke University Press 1998).

Langton R, *Sexual Solipsism: Philosophical Essays on Pornography and Objectification* (Oxford University Press 2009).

Lehman P, *Pornography: Film and Culture* (Rutgers University Press 2006).

MacKinnon C, *Feminism Unmodified: Discourses on Life and Law* (Harvard University Press 1987).

—— *Toward a Feminist Theory of the State* (Harvard University Press 1989).

—— and Andrea Dworkin (eds), *In Harm's Way: The Pornography Civil Rights Hearing* (Harvard University Press 1997).

—— *Are Women Human?: And Other International Dialogues* (Harvard University Press 2007).

Mill J S, *On Liberty* (Hackett Publishing 1978).

—— *The Subjection of Women* (Hackett Publishing 1988).

Mulvey L, 'Visual Pleasure and Narrative Cinema' in Leo Braudy and Marshall Cohen (eds), *Film Theory and Criticism* (Oxford University Press 1999).

Nussbaum M, *Sex and Social Justice* (Oxford University Press 1999).

Ross W (tr), *Aristotle: The Nicomachean Ethics* (Lesley Brown ed, Oxford University Press 2009).

Shimizu C, *The Hypersexuality of Race: Performing Asian/American Women on Screen and Scene* (Duke University Press 2007).

—— and Tristan Taormino, Constance Penley, Mireille Miller-Young, *The Feminist Porn Book* (The Feminist Press 2013).

Steinem G, *Outrageous Acts and Everyday Rebellions* (New American Library 1983).

Sullivan R and Alan McKee, *Pornography: Structures, Agency and Performance* (Polity Press 2015).

Williams L, *Hard Core: Power, Pleasure, and the "Frenzy of the Visible"* (University of California Press 1999).

Young S, *Beyond Rawls: An Analysis of the Concept of Political Liberalism* (University Press of America 2002).

Zillmann D, *Connections Between Sexuality and Aggression* (Psychology Press 1998).

Articles and Essays

Backlash, 'Written Evidence to Home Affairs' (2016) <http://data.-parliament.uk/writtenevidence/committeeevidence.svc/evidencedocument/home-affairs-committee/prostitution/written/29058.html> accessed 22 March 2016.

Bartlett K, 'MacKinnon's Feminism: Power on Whose Terms?' (1987) 75 *California Law Review* 1559.

Corliss R, 'That Old Feeling when Porno was Chic' (2005) <http://content.time.com/time/arts/article/0,8599,1043267,00.html> accessed 21 March 2016.

Dworkin A, 'Pornography Happens to Women' (1993) <http://www.nostatusquo.com/ACLU/dworkin/PornHappens.html> accessed on 3 April 2016.

Dworkin R, 'Is There a Right to Pornography?' (1981) *Oxford Journal of Legal Studies* 177.

—— 'Women and Pornography' (1993) *New York Review* 39.

Dyzenhaus D, 'John Stuart Mill and the Harm of Pornography' (1992) *Ethics Journal* 534.

Eaton A, 'A Sensible Antiporn Feminism' (2007) *Ethics Journal* 674.

MacKinnon C, 'Not a Moral Issue' (1984) *2 Yale Law and Policy Review* 321.

—— 'Reflections on Sex Equality under Law' (1991) 100 *Yale Law Journal* 1281.

Manning J, 'US Senate Hearing: The Impact of Internet Pornography on Marriage and the Family' (2005) <s3.amazonaws.-com/thf_media/2010/pdf/ManningTST.pdf> accessed 21 March 2016.

Stone G, 'The Government must Leave to the People the Evaluation of Ideas' (2010) 77 *University of Chicago Law Review* 1219.

Internet Sources

Eyes C, 'Pornography Statistics' (2015) <http://www.covenanteyes.com/lemonade/wp-content/uploads/2013/02/2015-porn-stats-covenant-eyes.pdf> accessed 21 March 2016.

Johnson R, 'Kant's Moral Philosophy', *The Stanford Encyclopedia of Philosophy* (Summer edition, 2014) <http://plato.stanford.edu/entries/kant-moral/> accessed 21 March 2016.

Taormino T, 'What is Feminist Porn?' (2013) <http://www.cosmopolitan.com/sex-love/news/a16343/tristan-taormino-feminist-porn-interview/> accessed 22 March 2016.

Van Mill D, 'Freedom of Speech', *The Stanford Encyclopedia of Philosophy* (Spring edition 2015) <http://plato.stanford.edu/entries/freedom-speech/> accessed 21 March 2016.

Case Comment: *Harb v HRH Prince Abdul Aziz Bin Fahd Bin Abdul Aziz* [2016] EWCA Civ 556: Judicial Apparent Bias and How It Affects the Parties

Konstantinos Georgiadis[1]

Even though the judge's behaviour could give rise to apparent bias against counsel of the defendant, the Court of Appeal in Harb, decided that the High Court judge's behaviour did not give rise to apparent bias - giving two arguments for their decision. This case comment will examine these arguments, eventually concluding that they are ultimately unconvincing. While it can be assumed that the aim of the judgement is to protect judges from frivolous and unsubstantiated claims, the judgment risks going too far and undermining public confidence in the judicial system. These arguments should be reconsidered to recognise that in some circumstances, a judge's behaviour towards counsel should be seen as apparent bias against the parties.

Keywords: Harb v Prince Abdul Aziz, Apparent Bias, Bias against Counsel

---

[1]LLM candidate, University of Leicester; Copy Editor, *Legal Issues Journal*.

1. Introduction

The England and Wales Court of Appeal (Civil Division) in *Harb v HRH Prince Abdul Aziz Bin Fahd Bin Abdul Aziz*[2] decided that

> ...the objective and fair-minded observer...would conclude that there was a real possibility that the judge was biased against all members of...Chambers, at least for a short period of time...[but] the observer would not conclude *without more* that there was a real possibility that this bias would affect the judge's determination of the issues in a case in which a party was represented by a member of...Chambers.[3]

Harb is the latest contribution to the state of the law in England and Wales regarding apparent judicial bias against counsel that is unrelated to the parties. The Court of Appeal reached this decision on two grounds as discussed below.

2. Apparent Bias

Public confidence in decision-making bodies, such as national courts, is contingent on the integrity of these systems;[4] the right to a fair trial (as described in multiple national and international instruments[5]) requires access to an 'independent and impartial tribunal'[6], with a biased tribunal producing a 'double evil': an evil against the party, whose human rights are being violated, and against society at large when public confidence in that decision-making system is compromised. Consequently, there is a need for

---

[2][2016] EWCA Civ 556.

[3]Ibid, [74] (Lord Dyson) (emphasis in original).

[4]Mark Elliot, Robert Thomas, *Public Law* (OUP 2014) 464.

[5]Including *inter alia* the European Convention on Human Rights (Article 6) and the International Covenant on Civil and Political Rights ('ICCPR') (Article 14).

[6]Article 14 ICCPR.

clear and sensible rules on whether a tribunal is, or has been, biased, however, proving that a judge was influenced by, for example, a financial stake in the outcome of a case is impossible without access to their private thoughts and records. For this reason, English Courts have developed a rule for 'apparent' bias.

Such a rule for apparent bias originates from the 1924 case of *R v Sussex Justices, ex p McCarthy.*[7] The Defendant, McCarthy, had caused a traffic accident where he collided with another vehicle. Police proceedings were initiated against McCarthy in the Magistrates court for driving in a manner dangerous to the public. The Complainant, also initiated civil proceedings against McCarthy for damages. The issue at large was that the Clerk in the criminal hearing for the Defendant was a member of the law firm representing the Complainant in civil proceedings. The clerk joined the magistrates when they retired to make their decision, and even though protested that his advice was not consulted upon, the Defendant was nevertheless convicted. On appeal, the conviction was quashed on the grounds that the Clerk, considering his connection to the case, should not have been present when the Judges were making their decision. Even though the judges made their conclusion without consulting the Clerk in question,[8] Lord Hewart held that 'justice should not only be done, but should manifestly and undoubtedly be *seen to be done*'[9], quashing the conviction on the grounds of apparent bias. The rule has evolved since then and the modern test for apparent bias in English law is found in the 2002 case of *Porter v McGill*: 'the question is whether the fair-minded and informed observer, having considered the facts, would conclude that there was a real possibility that the tribunal was biased'.[10]

---

[7][1924] 1 K.B. 256.

[8]Ibid, 259 (Lord Hewart CJ).

[9]Ibid, (emphasis added).

[10]*Porter v Magill* [2002] 2 AC 357 [103] (Lord Hope).

3. *Harb v HRH Prince Abdul Aziz Bin Fahd Bin Abdul Aziz*: Facts

Peter Smith J, the judge in *Harb,* decided that the parties did have an enforceable agreement (as the Claimant alleged), finding the Defendant liable. The Defendant appealed on five grounds, and under the fifth ground of the Appeal, the Defendant in *Harb* argued that the judge 'was apparently biased against the [Defendant]'.[11] This comment focuses on that issue.

The allegation of apparent bias stemmed from a letter, sent by Peter Smith J, to one of the heads of Blackstone Chambers - the Chambers of Lord Pannick QC, Mr. Ian Mill QC, and Ms. Shaheed Fatima QC, all of whom represented the defendant in *Harb*.

Lord Pannick QC wrote an article for *The Times* in September 2015, after the *Harb* hearing, but before the judge handed down his judgment criticising the judge's controversial[12] behaviour in the previous case of *Emerald Supplies Ltd v British Airways*[13]. The Article concluded:

> Litigants are entitled to a better service than this. The reputation of our legal system is damaged by such behaviour. The Lord Chief Justice should consider whether action to address Mr Justice Peter Smith's injudicious conduct has, like his luggage, been delayed for too long.[14]

---

[11] *Harb*, [17].

[12] 'High Court judge under investigation over British Airways luggage rant' (21 September 2015) *The Telegraph* <http://www.telegraph.co.uk/news/uknews/law-and-order/11879204/High-Court-judge-under-investigation-over-British-Airways-luggage-rant.html> accessed 20 June 2016.

[13] [2015] EWHC 2201 (Ch).

[14] David Pannick, 'A case about luggage with a great deal of judicial baggage' (3 September 2015) *The Times* <http://www.thetimes.co.uk/tto/law/columnists/article4545584.ece> accessed 20 June 2016.

In December 2015, after the *Harb* judgment was handed down, Peter Smith J wrote a letter to one of the heads of Blackstone Chambers. Calling Lord Pannick's article 'outrageous', and stating that the article 'has been extremely damaging to Blackstone Chambers within the Chancery Division', concluding that: 'I do not wish to be associated with Chambers that have people like Pannick in it.'[15] In their appeal, the Defendant argued that 'the fair-minded observer would consider that there was a real possibility that the final judgment was influenced by the article.'[16]

4. Judgement of the Court of Appeal

The Court of Appeal found that there were 'serious' deficiencies in the trial judge's decision, remitting the case to the High Court for re-trial.[17] In light of this, the Court of Appeal, seen no need to determine whether apparent bias existed or not. Although it did comment on the issue given the weight of the allegation, it found no apparent bias,[18] concluding that the *Porter v Magill* test was not satisfied for the following two reasons.

First, the Court was prepared to assume that the 'informed and fair-minded observer' would conclude that there was a real possibility that the judge was biased against all members of Blackstone Chambers, at least temporarily.[19] The same observer wrote that the Court would not conclude 'without more'[20] that there was a real possibility this bias would affect the judge's determination of the issues in this case.

The Court of Appeal supported this conclusion with two points. The first was that the 'fair-minded and informed observer' is not to be confused with the litigant - as the litigant 'lacks the objectivity

[15]*Harb,* [53].
[16]Ibid*,* [61].
[17]Ibid*,* [48].
[18]Ibid*,* [77].
[19]Ibid*,* [74].
[20]Ibid*,* (emphasis in original).

which is the hallmark of the fair-minded observer'[21], and that '[most] litigants are likely to oppose anything that they perceive might imperil their prospects of success'.[22] The Court illustrated this point using the case of *Helow v Secretary of State for the Home Department*[23], where a Palestinian woman had her case refused by Lord Ordinary. Lord Ordinary was a member of the International Association of Jewish Lawyers and Jurists, whose journal had published 'a number of extremely pro-Israeli articles'.[24] The House of Lords dismissed the woman's appeal for apparent bias. The House examined Lord Ordinary's relationship with the Association taking into account the fact that 'the judge was able to discount material she had read, reaching an impartial decision according to the law'.[25] While the applicant, in that case, could feel that there was an appearance of bias, based on the applicant's position and status, the 'objective and fair-minded observer' would not conclude that there was apparent bias.

The second point given by the Court was that 'even if a judge is irritated by or shows hostility towards an *advocate*', it does not mean that there is a real possibility for the judge's approach towards the parties to be affected. [26] Judges would not let their feelings about counsel affect their determination of a case as they are expected to follow their judicial oath.[27] The Court seems to argue that there is a distinction between bias toward counsel and bias toward parties, and judges are expected to maintain that distinction by virtue of their judicial oath.

The Court gave a further reason why the Appeal on apparent bias should fail, where Peter Smith J gave a provisional view that the Claimant should be successful, and handed over a draft judgement before the article was published. After that, the judge stated that any amendments he made were 'not material'.[28] The

[21]Ibid, [69].

[22]Ibid

[23][2008] UKHL 62.

[24]*Harb* [70].

[25]Ibid, [70].

[26]Ibid, [71].

[27]Ibid, [71].

[28]Ibid, [76]

Court of Appeal found it was 'fanciful to suppose'[29] that the judge made major changes to his assessment of the evidence simply as a reaction to the Article. The 'informed and fair-minded observer', therefore, would not conclude that there was a real possibility of bias in the assessment of the evidence

5. Analysis

First, the Court made a distinction between the opinion of the litigant and that of the informed and fair-minded observer, noting that the fair-minded observer does not share the concerns of the litigant. Such a problem with this approach is that it makes it difficult to see what would satisfy the informed and fair-minded observer. Some litigants may indeed have objectively well-founded concerns. Surely, in those situations, the informed and fair-minded observer would have to share the concerns of the litigant.

The Court used *Helow* to illustrate this point. But the Lord Ordinary in *Helow* was the member of an Association. She had not committed herself to the 'highly partisan' views presented in the publication of the Association or by the President of the Association - she had not even shown that she knew of these views.[30] Consequently, in that case, the House of Lords decided that the judge's membership alone was insufficient to make her biased. On the other hand, the judgements of both Lord Mance and Lord Rodger agreed that a judge expressing comments similar to those of the President of the Association *would* show an appearance of bias to the fair-minded and informed observer.[31]

Peter Smith J, having personally drafted and sent the letter in *Harb*, showed clear bias against Blackstone Chambers, and it could be argued that, compared to *Helow*, his behaviour is very much different to the behaviour of Lord Ordinary in that case - who had not written or expressed any opinions, and closer to the behaviour of the President of the Association, who had gone on

[29] Ibid

[30] *Helow* [53] (Lord Mance).

[31] Ibid, [17] (Lord Rodger), [53] (Lord Mance).

record expressing strong views on the subject. Taking this into consideration, *Helow* did not demonstrate that the litigant's concern may not be objective, as the Court of Appeal seeks to show. On the contrary, the contrast between *Helow* and *Harb* goes to show that litigants may have objective concerns that could be shared by the informed and fair-minded observer.

Second, the Court provided no sources for the claim that hostility towards an advocate does not affect his or her approach to the parties. The opinion was that a judge will be fair to the parties, irrespective of their biases towards counsel because they have taken a judicial oath. However, as mentioned by Lord Walker in *Helow*, the informed and fair-minded observer 'would be tending towards complacency if he treated the fact of having taken the judicial oath as a panacea'.[32]

Moreover, this reasoning divorces the party from their counsel. This distinction is untenable, as counsel is there to represent the interests of the parties. For example, it is clear that there is an appearance of bias when a judge or judicial assistant is also a partner in the firm acting against the defendant in another case (as was the case in *McCarthy*).

Third, the reasoning of the court that it was 'rather fanciful' and 'unrealistic' to suggest that the judge would make major changes to his judgment because of the article seem to suggest that the test for apparent bias is one of likelihood. However, the test talks of a real *possibility* of bias. Debating whether an action is likely or not, as the words 'fanciful' and 'unrealistic' seem to suggest, risks undermining the principle behind the apparent bias rule that justice must be 'seen to be done'. The Court of Appeal conceded that the judge '*could* have amended his draft judgement after reading the Article.'[33] Following *McCarthy* and *Porter*, if the judge *could* have done so, this should satisfy the test; whether he, in fact, did so should not be a consideration.

These are some of the objections that suggest this ruling may prove an unwelcome precedent in the future. Of course, considering that the Court felt it was 'unnecessary' to actually determine the issue, it could be argued that the ruling on apparent bias

---

[32]Ibid, [27] (Lord Walker).

[33]*Harb* [76].

forms part of the *obiter dictum* of the case, and as such is not binding. It does, however, retain its 'persuasive' status, and the objections noted here should be taken into account in future cases.

6. Conclusion

After *Harb*, the current state of the law on apparent bias of a judge against counsel is uncertain. The Court decided that hostility or aggression towards counsel by a judge is, by itself, insufficient to show an appearance of bias. This decision is sensible in practice: judges should be able to perform their everyday duties without constant fear of being accused of bias.

On the other hand, there should be a line where, if a judge is hostile or aggressive enough towards counsel, the 'fair-minded and objective observer' would find a real possibility of bias. While the Court of Appeal did not recognise such an exception, the 'public confidence' element of apparent bias dictates it, as justice should be 'seen to be done'. There is a need for further research to find specific instances where this line might lie. For example, the Supreme Court of New Zealand found that the fact that a judge owed a substantial amount of money to counsel in a shared business venture was sufficient to show apparent bias.[34] For the time being, it can only be said that Peter Smith J's letter, though 'shocking … and disgraceful,'[35] as the Court of Appeal wrote, was not explicit enough as to cross the line into apparent bias.

---

[34] *Saxmere Co Ltd v Wool Board Disestablishment Co Ltd (No2)* [2009] NZSC 122, 1 NZLR 76 (SC).
[35] *Harb* [68].

Case Comment: *Heneghan v Manchester Dry Docks Ltd*: The Limits of the Fairchild Exception

Jonathan Mellor [1]

The decision in Heneghan v Manchester Dry Docks Ltd *represents a further link in the complex chain of causation in negligence cases. Lord Dyson MR in the Court of Appeal, who delivered the main judgment, considered several issues pertinent to causation: the uses that can be made of epidemiological evidence, the application of the material contribution in* Bonnington Castings Ltd v Wardlaw, *and the limits of the material contribution to risk rule in* Fairchild v Glenhaven Funeral Services. *Lord Dyson MR supported the use of epidemiological evidence in proving on the balance of probabilities that lung cancer was caused by asbestos exposure as opposed to smoking, and held that the Fairchild rule could apply to cases featuring a similar instance of scientific uncertainty as that which gave rise to the rule itself. The latter development represents a principled move based on Weinrib's thesis of remedial continuity as the theoretical rationale for applying an exception to the but-for test of causation in both mesothelioma and lung cancer cases.*

Keywords: causation, material contribution, asbestos, lung cancer, apportionment, *Fairchild*, *Heneghan*

---

[1] BA Jurisprudence, University of Oxford; Bachelor of Civil Law Candidate at St Hughes College, University of Oxford.

1. Introduction

Rightly or wrongly, tort law has tended to remain faithful to the notion of proving causation by establishing that a defendant's breach of duty was, on the balance of probabilities, a but-for cause of the claimant's injury. In addition to the developments in the doctrine of material contribution to risk in *Bonnington Castings Ltd v Wardlaw*[2] and *Bailey v Ministry of Defence*,[3] the main flight from this orthodoxy has been the *McGhee v National Coal Board*[4] and *Fairchild v Glenhaven Funeral Services Ltd*[5] material increase in risk doctrine. The case of *Heneghan v Manchester Dry Docks Ltd*[6] has developed the subject matter further and introduced limits to the doctrine.

2. The Facts

Mr James Heneghan contracted lung cancer as a result of his occupational exposure to asbestos dust and fibres throughout his working life. He was employed by the six defendant employers between 1961 and 1974, and from a lifetime exposure of 133.1 fibres/ml years, these employers were responsible for a cumulative total of 46.9 fibres/ml years, or 35.2%. The individual exposures for which the individual defendants were responsible ranged from 2.5% to 10.1%. A threshold of 25 fibres/ml year is sufficient to permit the inference that an individual's lung cancer is attributable to the asbestos. As all six defendants admitted their negligence in relation to these exposures, the issue before the Court of Appeal was whether each of those defendants were jointly and severally liable for the whole of the damages or proportionately liable for their contribution to the cumulative total.

---

[2] [1956] UKHL 1.

[3] [2008] EWCA Civ 883.

[4] [1972] 3 All ER 1008.

[5] [2002] UKHL 22.

[6] [2016] EWCA Civ 86.

At first instance, the defendant argued that the question of causation ought to be settled by the rule in *Fairchild v Glenhaven Funeral Services Ltd*, with the corollary question of recovery to be governed by the decision in *Barker v Corus UK Ltd*[7] on proportionate recovery. S 3 of the Compensation Act 2006, which implemented joint and several liability for *Fairchild* cases, applies only to mesothelioma claims, and so *Barker* remains the authority at common law. It was, of course, the unknown aetiology of mesothelioma and its incidence in employees who had sustained multiple asbestos fibre exposures that constituted the facts of *Fairchild*, and prompted the strengthening of the *McGhee* causation rule in that case Mesothelioma is a severely debilitating condition with no prospect of recovery, and was thus an issue perceived to be of sufficient importance to prompt both judicial developments and the legislative response in the Compensation Act. The presence of similar scientific uncertainty in *Heneghan* in the context of a serious illness whose origin was the claimant's industrial employment made the case ripe for the application of the *Fairchild* rule.

The claimant, meanwhile, sought to argue that joint and several liability could be based on each defendant's material contribution to the development of lung cancer. At trial, however, Jay J rejected the position of the claimant's expert witness, Dr Rudd, who was of the view that there was a positive relationship between asbestos exposure and damage to lung tissue. Rather, Jay J maintained that the question was still one of increased *risk* in each defendant's case. This was because the epidemiological and scientific evidence did not permit the conclusion that on the balance of probabilities the exposure *contributed* to the defendant's lung cancer. [8] The evidence could only make a statistical judgment based on the quantum of exposure and the concomitant risk of the disease arising, and could not make an assessment linked to the physical presence of dust deposits in the lung tissue.[9] In essence, what was rejected at trial was the claimant's argument that the fibres from each source were likely to have

[7][2006] UKHL 20.

[8][2014] EWHC 4190 (QB) at para. 30.

[9]*Henghan* (first instance) at para. 63.

played a part in the carcinogenic process and that each defendant made a material contribution to the contraction of the deceased's lung cancer. Jay J held that the *Fairchild* doctrine was not limited to mesothelioma cases, and applied to this instance of lung cancer to allow the claimant to recover from the defendants on a pro rata basis.

3. The Court of Appeal

Lord Dyson MR adopted a two-stage inquiry into the causation question. He first asked the '*what*' question, and applied epidemiological evidence to establish that the cumulative exposure for which the six defendants were responsible had more than doubled the risk of lung cancer developing. The baseline risk of developing lung cancer was 0.5 per cent. This was increased to 2 per cent by the deceased's smoking, and to 10 per cent by the exposure to asbestos. This meant that the exposure had resulted in a fivefold increase in the deceased's chances of contracting lung cancer. This exercise proved that it was more likely than not that a tortfeasor caused the injury and that, on the balance of probabilities, the deceased's lung cancer had been caused by this asbestos exposure as opposed to the smoking of cigarettes.

The second question was the '*who*' question In this regard, the same point of contention which had arisen at trial was considered, namely that the gap in scientific knowledge in relation to lung cancer's aetiology would not allow the conclusion that each defendant had materially contributed to the onset of the disease.[10] The claimant's argument, however, was that the facts amounted to a case similar to *Bonnington Castings v Wardlaw Ltd. Bonnington* involved the partly negligent and partly non-negligent exposures to silica dust which were capable of causing pneumoconiosis, a lung disease capable of being caused by the inhalation of a range of types of dust. It could not be established that, on the balance of probabilities, the condition would have arisen but for the defendant's negligence. However, it was held that the negli-

[10] *Heneghan* at para. 42.

gent exposure to dust had materially contributed to the claimant developing the disease. The principle was established that where the defendant's breach is one of a number of agents which bring about a specific harm or loss, and so long as the defendant's breach is not *de minimis* and materially contributed to the outcome, they can be held liable for that outcome.

The Master of the Rolls did not accept that any individual defendant's exposure could be said to have materially contributed to the carcinogenesis, and hence *Bonnington* could not be applied to the second stage.[11] He made it clear that there was a distinction to be made between a material contribution to an injury and a material increase to the risk of an injury.[12] This marked the different territory of the *Bonnington* case law on one hand, and the *McGhee* and *Fairchild* case law on the other. The statistical data only allowed a quantification of each defendant's contribution to the increased risk, and would therefore involve the extension of the *Fairchild* principle, which requires claimants to show only that the defendant's exposure materially increased the risk that they would develop mesothelioma.

Lord Dyson MR then stated that the conditions for the application of *Fairchild* to the present case were satisfied:

- All defendants had conceded that they had breached their duty of care;
- All defendants had increased the risk that the deceased would contract lung cancer;
- All defendants had exposed the deceased to the same agency that was implicated in causation;

Medical science was unable to determine which, if any, of the defendants should be attributed the exposure which ultimately resulted in the cancer.[13]

He argued that '[t]here can be no objection in principle to extending it to situations which are not materially different from

[11] Ibid at para. 46.
[12] Ibid at para. 45.
[13] Ibid at para. 47.

Fairchild',[14] continuing: '[i]ndeed, principle requires that in a situation which is truly analogous to that considered in that case, the *Fairchild* exception should be applied. Otherwise the law in this area would be inconsistent and incoherent.'[15]

4. Comment

4.1 The first stage

The first stage of the two-step exercise is concerned with proving that, on the balance of probabilities, the claimant has been the victim of someone's tort. It is suggested that doing so sidesteps the necessity of complying with the otherwise arbitrary single agent rule designed to limit *Fairchild* that was formulated in *Wilsher v Essex Area Health Authority.*[16] This step coheres with Sarah Green's Necessary Breach analysis,[17] which firstly asks whether it is more likely than not that a defendant's breach caused the claimant's harm, and if so, whether the effect of that breach was operative when the harm occurred. She explains that the first stage shows that 'the claimant would have been better off without any breaches of duty', and that the second stage is about ensuring that compensation comes from 'those defendants whose breaches of duty have made an actual contribution to the claimant's state at trial'.[18] One might question the need for this first stage, given that the second stage is merely about proving liability for increasing the risk. In this respect, the first stage of the Necessary Breach Analysis relies on at least one of a bundle of tortious acts being necessary to divert the plaintiff from her normal course of events. This makes it more likely than not that *a* tortious act caused the claimant's injury.

---

[14]Ibid at para. 48.

[15]Ibid

[16][1988] AC 1074.

[17]Green, *Causation in Negligence* (Oxford: Hart Publishing, 2015), 2.

[18]Ibid 5.

However, as Lord Dyson MR admitted,[19] doubts had been raised in *Sienkiewicz*[20] about the validity of using epidemiological data to establish that a risk had been doubled and thus that a factor was a cause on the balance of probabilities, but saw no such problems in the case before him. Lord Phillips in that case noted that 'statistical evidence may be an inadequate basis upon which to found a finding of causation'[21] owing to the questionable reliability and concomitant uncertainty as to the adequacy of the data. However, and in the context of differentiating one potential agent (asbestos) from another (smoking), Lord Dyson was confident that using epidemiological data to show that the cumulative asbestos exposures more than doubled the risk of developing lung cancer was a valid means of proving on the balance of probabilities that the cause of the deceased's lung cancer was a breach of duty. Although he was not explicit in his reasoning as to why there was 'no doubt as to the validity of applying [epidemiological evidence] to answer the first question',[22] Lord Dyson was more forthright in his speech in *Sienkiewicz*, stating that there was 'no *a priori* reason why, if the epidemiological evidence is cogent enough, it should not be sufficient to enable a claimant to prove his case without more'.[23] He earlier suggested that to do so would be a 'policy choice'[24] based on the quality of the evidence used, given that the courts do not insist on 'absolute certainty' in any case.

4.2 The second stage

The incremental extension of *Fairchild* in the second '*who*' stage of the causation exercise is justified. Lord Brown in *Sienkiewicz* warned gravely against the extension of the rule, arguing that its principled application beyond the facts of *Fairchild* was a perilous exercise, and suggested that it ought to be tied down to mesothe-

---

[19] *Heneghan* at para. 8.
[20] [2011] UKSC 10.
[21] Ibid at para. 96.
[22] *Heneghan* at para. 8.
[23] *Sienkiewicz* at para. 222.
[24] Ibid at para. 219.

lioma cases alone.[25] But Jay J in *Heneghan* considered lung cancer and mesothelioma to be 'legally indistinguishable'[26] on the basis that the scientific uncertainty of the aetiology in both instances prevents a claimant establishing but-for causation on the balance of probabilities. Thus, both instances require the fashioning of a rule less apt to throwing up false negatives. It is worth noting that the *Fairchild* exception was actually the progeny of *McGhee*, which concerned dermatitis. This suggests that arguments attempting to limit *Fairchild* based on specific characteristics of mesothelioma are unfounded. *McGhee*, the original case to base causation on a material increase in risk, was perhaps initially underappreciated in its novelty. This was a state of affairs that resulted from Lord Bridge's judgement in *Wilsher*; he denied that *McGhee* had articulated a new principle of law and was of the opinion that it was merely a 'robust and pragmatic' inference of factual causation from the evidence.[27] Lord Hoffman in *Barker*, however, confirmed the reinterpretation of *McGhee* as 'an approved application of the *Fairchild* exception'.[28]

Moreover, Lord Bingham in *Fairchild* itself argued that:

> [T]here is a strong policy argument in favour of compensating those who have suffered grave harm, at the expense of their employers who owed them a duty of care to protect them against that very harm and failed to do so, when the harm can only have been caused by breach of that duty and when science does not permit the victim accurately to attribute, as between several employers, the precise responsibility for the harm he has suffered.[29]

Lord Phillips in *Sienkiewicz* also envisaged a principled development, and advocated for its extension to the situation where 'one could postulate with confidence that the extent of the contribution

---

[25] Ibid at paras. 184-86.

[26] *Heneghan* (first instance) at para. 81.

[27] *Wilsher* at para. 1090.

[28] *Barker* at para. 13.

[29] *Fairchild* at para. 33.

of a defendant to the victim's exposure to asbestos precisely reflected the likelihood that his breach of duty had caused the victim's disease'.[30]

4.3 Broader implications

As a matter of theory, the extension of the principle coheres with a satisfactory conception of corrective justice. Weinbrib has spoken in favour of exceptions to but-for causation in instances where the claimant is the victim of a tort on the balance of probabilities, but where *particular* liability on the part of a single defendant cannot be proven. He posits that the thesis of remedial continuity provides the answer.[31] The thesis treats the remedial right to damages not as an altogether separate response to the substantive right to bodily integrity, but as a continuation, surviving in a different form post-injury and assuming the shape of a right to receive from the tortfeasor the equivalent of what was injured. Consequently, each tortfeasor can be viewed as having either (i) infringed the claimant's substantive right by causing the injury, or (ii) prevented the claimant from establishing a claim against whichever defendant in fact performed (i) by contributing to the uncertainty preventing factual differentiation of defendants, and therefore hindering the legal mechanism by which the claimant would receive remedial damages. Both defendants have created a wrongful risk to the bodily security of the claimant. This justification for *Fairchild* is neither disease-specific nor dependent on troublesome arithmetic; it rather offers an elegant conceptual solution to problems of causal uncertainty featuring multiple defendants.

[30] *Sienkiewicz* at para. 105.

[31] Weinrib, 'Causal Uncertainty' (2016) 36 (1) Oxford Journal of Legal Studies 135, 145-149.

5. Conclusion

The judgment in *Heneghan* has pushed the law of causation onwards. The extension of the *Fairchild* rule to cases beyond mesothelioma tends towards the idea that the doctrine might become a generalised rule of causation. This may be used to remedy the potential injustices posed by scientific uncertainty and defendant indeterminacy in personal injury cases.

The United Kingdom Law Students Association Legal Issues is operated by volunteers and relies on donations.
To support the Journal or UKLSA in general, email president@uklsa.co.uk.

Website: www.uklsa.co.uk
Facebook: www.facebook.com/UKLSA
Twitter: https://twitter.com/UKLSA

www.ingramcontent.com/pod-product-compliance
Lightning Source LLC
LaVergne TN
LVHW050303210926
848481LV00014BA/805